Border Experiences with Evil

Personal accounts and interpretations with a view towards the best promise for life

Heinrich Bammann

VTR
Publications

The author wants to thank Klaudia Ringelman from Pretoria for her translation from the German book *Grenzerfahrungen des Bösen: Persönliche Erlebnisse und Deutungen mit Ausblick auf die beste Zusage des Lebens*.

ISBN 978-3-95776-110-1

VTR Publications
Gogolstr. 33, 90475 Nuremberg, Germany, http://www.vtr-online.com

Contents

Preface I

Heinrich Bammann proffers a recipe for successful resistance to the influence of evil spirits. Their apparent aim is to destroy his faith in God and thereby disrupt his ordered life. His presentation can be divided into two phases his personal struggle against, and triumph over evil spirits, and the seminal exposition of the power of god.

The reader is taken along a chronicle of personal experiences with evil spirits resident in the church mission house in *Ga-Rankuwa*, Pretoria (Republic of South Africa), as well as the itinerant evil forces that dogged his travels in the mainly *Batswana* populated Western Diocese of the Lutheran Church.

Secondly, he demonstrates the power of God. Trust in the mercy and grace of the Lord relieves one from situations that seem hopeless to overcome. The Christian must accept and rise above the challenges thrown at him as Jesus did when the devil tested his faith.

Since attention by evil spirits seems to be selective, it might be asked whether certain individuals are prone to eliciting this attention. On the other hand, are there individuals "gifted" to recognising the presence of supernatural forces? The debate will rage on.

Jacob Ikageng Monnakgotla

Preface II

In the fight against the power of evil, one is never only confronted by a human being. "For we do not wrestle against flesh and blood, but against the rulers, against the authorities, against the cosmic powers over this present darkness, against the spiritual forces of evil in the heavenly places" – as the Bible expresses it (Ephesians 6:12). In our modern day and age, we struggle with this viewpoint. We are children of the Enlightenment, and during the Enlightenment people sang:

> "May the Praise of God for ever abound!
> No more Devil on earth to be found!
> But say, how was he reduced to naught?
> Undone by reason and rational thought!"[1]

But is this optimism really justified? Or is it rather flippant? Does this optimism not repress certain experiences we ourselves encounter today?

Our use of language is more knowing, more serious in this regard. Modern-day phrases still refer to certain depravities as "devilries". Certain situations elicit from us the exclamation: "What the devil is going on?" An adjective like "bedevilled" and a verb like "bedevil" also exist in our language.

It was Johann Wolfgang von Goethe, of all people, who penned the much-quoted lines: "These folk wouldn't feel the devil, even if he'd got them dangling by the neck."[2]

In his book, Heinrich Bammann introduces us to the world of the Batswana people, as well as a number of related tribes in Southern Africa. What he shares with us are first and foremost not theories, but experiences he had while doing his missionary work in various

---

[1] *'Gott sei ewig Preis und Ehr! Es gibt keinen Teufel mehr! Ja, wo ist er denn geblieben?' Die Vernunft hat ihn vertrieben!* – The translation of this verse is the translator's own.

[2] *'Den Teufel spürt das Völkchen nie, und wenn sie am Kragen hätte'* – from Johann Wolfgang von Goethe's *Faust* I.

congregations of this tribe for more than twenty years, and interpreting these experiences in the light of the New Testament.

His account will doubtlessly elicit very diverse responses from readers. But whatever judgement an individual person forms on the depicted phenomena: the realisation will soon set in that, whoever wishes to bear up against such phenomena, will require more than an enlightened denial or a rational interpretation of the facts. One's enlightened denial of the demonic origin of certain experiences will not suffice. The question of resilience takes on a crucial meaning: Where will the patience, courage, trust and ability for me to bear up against these phenomena come from?

With his book, it is not Heinrich Bammann's intention at all to make us afraid, but rather to turn our eyes to Him, who has long since emerged victorious from this struggle: Jesus Christ, who has come to "destroy the works of the devil." Because of His victory, all devilment has come to naught. May this faith be especially strengthened by the book, so that we do not dwell on the harm that is wrought by forces of evil, but turn our eyes to Him, whose victory has been decided and will last for ever.

Reinhard Deichgräber

I. Introduction

I had my experiences with forces of evil while I was serving as missionary in South Africa. These experiences occurred many years ago. Only now have I finally been able to bring myself to publish them. Does the fact that they occurred quite a number of years ago mean that similar phenomena no longer occur today? That statement cannot be made. At the beginning of this year I revisited the areas where I used to do my missionary work. I stayed for a few months, during which two of my African friends told me of cases in which they had only recently experienced the horrors of evil.

But what experiences did I have? Before I go into those, a couple of thoughts that may point towards the subject at hand. The house of the missionary is apparently haunted. Is that to be believed? Spirits have sneaked into the house. What is going on? Ghost stories relating to parsonages are not that uncommon. Churches also have their share of ghost stories. These kinds of stories can be found in previous centuries, but surely not in our enlightened day and age.

When a place is haunted, when hostile spirits terrify and unsettle our lives, we no longer see the humorous side of it. We might laugh about it afterwards when the haunting has stopped. Spirits often deal with people who have a certain aversion towards a particular individual, and therefore trigger the haunting in a secretive way. Since the phenomena that I am writing about obey their own laws, there is always a certain amount of danger involved for us humans. As a rule, the intentions of a haunting spirit are not good; they are evil. By virtue of my experiences I have assigned a particular kind of evil to these phenomena. It is for this reason that, in the following, I rather speak of evil, of a power of evil or of evil spirits rather than a haunting, by which I mean not only ghosts, but every kind of spirit.

Each manifestation of evil presents itself in a different way. An evil phenomenon can also be assessed from different angles. Each occurrence or manifestation of an evil force should be individually investigated and examined.

All evil starts out as something insignificant. Rising from below, it can escalate to become well-nigh unbearable. If it is detected in its early stages and directed into appropriate channels, or if a satisfactory explanation is provided in the event of greater damage having been inflicted, it is possible to contain it. Then it is weakened and soon loses its significance as being something evil. However, if the evil has transformed into something powerful, it can become very dangerous. Then it becomes almost impossible for the individual who is confronted by it to extricate him- or herself from it.

For many modern people, the evil as I present it here has already lost its meaning a long time ago. A number of good friends of mine acknowledged as much. For them, it may have existed in the early Middle Ages, during the Reformation period, and during times when humans played their wicked games with dark magical forces. French Revolution, Enlightenment, Industrialisation, and all the other factors that have contributed to the emergence of modern civilisation, have led to the disappearance of the notion of evil from the world of modern man. Remnants of it make the odd appearance now and then, or surface in foreign religions.

There are other people in my circle of acquaintances who take the concept of evil very seriously. They are alert to the power of Satan. They fear evil, and some of them have had personal encounters with it in one way or another.

Both groups refer to themselves as Christians. They differ fundamentally in their attitude towards evil. Both groups nevertheless pray the same words in The Lord's Prayer, where it says: "… and lead us not into temptation, but deliver us from evil."

If we now concern ourselves with the subject of evil, an objection could be raised by the one side: Why should people nowadays still concern themselves at all with the subject of evil and the occult – as it is called in more extreme cases –, since it is only a small number of people who are affected by it, and besides, evil hardly features anymore in modern life? The other side could also raise its objection: One should not get involved with evil whatsoever. Just by putting oneself in close proximity of evil puts one in danger already.

I find it difficult to argue with the first group of people. They laugh at my experiences and are unwilling to be convinced by the experiences of others. We can compare those people with Thomas (John 20:25), who told the other disciples of Jesus: "Unless I see ... I will not believe." I can relate more to the second group. These people understand my concern. My advice to both groups is not to be inquisitive where evil is concerned.

The occupation with evil can most certainly cause a person harm. Examples thereof can be found amongst young people, who just once wanted to risk slightly more than others in an exotic or supernatural way by attracting these hostile powers, and subsequently were unable to get rid of them. There are adults, too, who wanted to find out whether Satan, about whom the church goes on so much, actually exists, and whether he has any power at all, only to succumb to him after having come into contact with the powers of evil.[3]

And there are parapsychologists who have spent their lives dealing with the virus of evil, but who have not gauged their own resistance against it realistically enough, so that the spirits did not let them reach the natural end of their lives. If someone spends too much time in observing evil as an object of study they can be infected by it themselves. One of the so-called "ghost hunters" is said to also have returned on one occasion after his death.[4]

Evil is cited frequently in the Bible. It rejects evil as being inimical to God. The Old Testament, in particular, points out that evil is to be shunned. Instead of evil, the believer should do good (Prov 3:7; Ps 34:15). It should however not be underestimated that an enemy – as evil presents itself to humans – can only be overcome in the event that this enemy has become known through his onslaughts and assaults. An enemy can only be wounded and his assaults only be thwarted if he has been previously observed.

At this point, devout people could raise the objection: Our Lord didn't gather information either in order to prepare himself for his own temptation. The Lord only relied on the power of his heavenly Father. Should Christians therefore not just simply ignore evil? If it should then attack them, they must simply relinquish the battle with evil to the Lord. After all, the Lord has overcome evil once and for all.

---

[3] Cf. Lee, R., Beware the Devil. A True Story of Deliverance from Evil. Aylesbury: Marshall, Morgan and Scott, 1983.

[4] Farsen, p. 136.

Yes, if it were as easy as people make it out to be, that would indeed be the best way to go about it. But it is also well known that unresolved and often apparently unresolvable interpersonal relationships bring a great deal of evil into the world, so that the finger of blame should not only be pointed at the devil.

It must be emphasised that evil can gain a considerable amount of power. The part that humans can play where evil is concerned should however not be underestimated. And it will also be demonstrated how evil can be overcome. Since evil can manifest itself in many different ways, this book makes no claims in being exhaustive on the subject. The number of personal examples that I use to demonstrate evil as well as to put forward some kind of explanation is a small one, compared to the many manifestations of evil. But that does not make them any less important.

The described manifestations that have occurred provide an insight into the sorcery and magic of Africa. Moreover, on one occasion the power of evil, which is usually active in an indirect way, becomes active out of its own accord. It follows in the wake of sorcery and insinuates itself wherever sorcery and magic have chosen their point of entry.

Now and again I refer to Europe by way of comparison. I cite books that posit my experiences. Since I not only had my experiences in South Africa – a country where English is spoken – but also wrote them down in that country, it was an obvious choice for me, over and above the German secondary literature, to primarily consult English literature for comparative purposes in this regard, and to quote suitable passages from these.

It is widely known that hostile spirits, too, have not simply disappeared from modern life. In many parts of the world they are being attracted by magical powers. To this day sorcery and magical powers are being deployed in Africa and elsewhere if someone finds him- or herself in a compromised position towards someone else. They are also being deployed if one person wants to demonstrate his or her power or, for reasons of self-interest, wishes to escape from daily life for a while to withdraw incognito into an arcane, immaterial world of spirit power inspired by magic.[5]

---

[5] The latter e.g. occurs when witches hold nocturnal get-togethers or make house visits but do not wish to be seen.

Sorcery and magic are not a vestige of primitive people. Witchcraft and sorcery have occurred time and again throughout the civilised countries of Europe. What is more, a recurring manifestation of these powers can be discerned, especially in recent times. In his book *"Okkultismus"*, F. Janzen writes: "The return of sorcerers, witches and healers is noteworthy."[6] According to Janzen's observations and depictions, four points can be listed as an indication of the fact that modern people are seduced by and drawn to those hostile and otherworldly powers. The four points made evident by Janzen and underscored by me are the following: 1. "In fanciful rituals accompanied by poetic words, symbolic acts and magical paraphernalia, the power of nature is celebrated with the objective of aligning oneself with it." 2. "In all of this, people want to find their true will." 3. "It is a matter of channelling cosmic energies into the body...." 4. "In doing so, the participants must discover 'submerged' abilities and 'expand their consciousness'."[7] Janzen's account describes instances where modern people wish to experience religion in a new way, transcending the barriers of everyday life into a realm that opens a door to otherworldly forces that, for their part, are supposed to unleash new powers. While Janzen's cogitations are strongly informed by esotericism and spiritualism, the manifestations in Africa can almost exclusively be ascribed to African tradition and religion.

The renewed orientation by Europeans towards occult powers can have positive as well as negative consequences for the person involved. The former are usually short-lived. Generally, the negative aspects outweigh any positive aspect. Participation is initiated by the individual. For the most part, the individual controls the extent to which he or she wishes to attract these powers.

In Africa, those who are affected by these powers are the ones who suffer. They don't attract these powers themselves. Evil makes its ap-

---

[6] Op. cit., p. 17-18. – 'Bemerkenswert ist die Wiederkehr der Magier, Hexen und Heiler.'

[7] 1. 'In phantasievollen Ritualen feiert man mit poetischen Worten, symbolhaften Handlungen und magischen Utensilien die Kräfte der Natur und will sich in ihr einordnen.' 2. 'In alledem will man seinen wahren Willen finden.' 3. 'Dabei geht es darum, kosmische Energien in den Körper zu leiten, ...' 4. 'Dabei sollen die Teilnehmer ‚verschüttete' Fähigkeiten entdecken und ihr Bewußtsein erweitern'.

pearance unexpectedly. The assault of evil is initiated by humans who very often form part of the immediate circle of relatives or friends. It emanates from the social environment. A burden is placed upon the person for whom the assault is intended. He or she suffers from an occult bondage from which they are unable to free themselves by their own efforts; subsequently they accept it as their fate.

There exists a certain manner by which magical powers can be deployed as an end in itself, and there are certain people who have accessed magical powers and are able to shapeshift. Through knowledge and appropriation of magical powers, witches are able to initiate their own transmission.

Janzen is also cognisant of the different kinds of sorcery and witchcraft. He differentiates between the less dangerous glimpse into the so-called otherworld on the one hand and the more dangerous utilisation of magic with the terms "receptive and active method."[8]

I may be given some credit for my attempt to present my own experiences with magical powers as objectively as I possibly can. I personally did not want the magic and the ensuing evil to happen. All the people in the area where I worked knew about it. It took me completely by surprise when I was confronted with it one day. This first encounter was still relatively harmless, as we will see later.

But I can probably not wash my hands of the circumstance that the one or other person, for whatever reason, became angry with me. Must they then respond with magical means? It is not my intention to exaggerate anything with the examples I am about to present, or to favour one case over another, or to bear a grudge against or discredit someone who got involved in a case. I have changed the names of the persons concerned to protect their families.

The examples I present here happened without my consent. One cannot take issue with evil. It proves itself to be a malignant force. More than ten years have now passed since I was last in conflict with a clandestine evil power, providing me with the necessary distance to integrate these things into an appropriate context.

---

[8] '...rezeptive und aktive Methode'.

Psychologists might raise objections to my examples, saying that they are all psychological in origin. One could argue with C. G. Jung: In a country where life and thought happens along collective lines, the collective unconscious operates on and demands outward manifestation. One could discard everything that easily.

Parapsychologists would probably analyse and assess the cases that have occurred, using the concept of 'psi' as key. For me the experiences constituted a very real power when they occurred, with very few means to confront it at my disposal, a power that I was ill-prepared for and that took me completely by surprise.

Finding an answer to the evil, hostile powers, and the process of shaking them off or to conquer them has been affected by confronting them by means of my own reflections, by the prayers of another missionary who was also my friend, and by the good forces of our heavenly Father who stood beside me.

The examples I offer occurred at various places. In the first example a bird is trained at midnight by hostile forces with a specific objective in mind.

II. The Manifestation of Evil

1. The bewitched night bird

a) The example

During an otherwise normal night I suddenly awake with a start. Between our house and the church, a bird is making unbearable shrieking noises into the night. Since it shows no signs of stopping its shrieking, I grab a torch and go out into the dark night. I shine a light into the thorn trees from where the unnatural shrieking has emanated. I can't see anything. Nothing special about that, one might ostensibly assume. It doesn't take long before the unusual bird utters its shrieks again, this time from another tree further away. From that distance it doesn't sound so loud anymore. During the following two nights the bird comes back again, each time at midnight. After that it disappeared for ever.

b) The analysis

The first rural congregation I was to minister to for a year as a temporary replacement for another missionary was situated in an area of flat bushveld, 40 km away from the nearest European town. The parsonage is about 90 years old. It had more rooms than I would be able to occupy by myself.

The incident with the night bird was no ordinary one. Therefore I had to give some thought to it. I remembered reading somewhere that a sorcerer has the power to send a bird at night to a place specified by him. Was this what had occurred here too? But what reason could there be to do such a thing?

I took my queries about this incident to an experienced missionary who had been born in the country. He was well versed in traditional African culture. What he told me confirmed my assumptions. Was the strange bird supposed to deliver a message to me? I seemed to have upset the indigenous community somehow with something I did. The community for its part responded in an age-old arcane way by despatching a bewitched night bird.

I pondered whether I could possibly have behaved in an inappropriate way. Had I committed a misdemeanour by regularly jogging in the evenings to get some physical exercise, only to return home after dark? I had always been actively involved in sports and was, amongst others, preparing to participate in a publicly announced marathon race. Had I committed a misdemeanour by slaughtering a diseased pig at midday? There were possibly a number of other things that attracted attention of which I am not aware. In any event, a close watch was kept on my civilised behaviour. What's more, there were people in my immediate vicinity who thought of my behaviour as deviating from their way of life.

I wish to add the following to the two mentioned examples of my behaviour: Because of the summer heat I had moved my jogging to the early evening hours. In doing so, I have frightened people. If a European person in Africa jogs through a settlement at dusk, this can lead to various associations among the indigenous people who accord greater weight to traditional life.

Seeing that the young people of the congregation had offered to help me to slaughter the pig, but could only do so after school, we decided to slaughter the pig around noon. But according to the notion of local medicine men a pig should not be slaughtered around noon. When the sun is at its zenith the ancestors are resting. Doing work around noon is frowned upon.

My ignorance and lack of heedfulness had induced some *Batswana* people in my vicinity to set a little retaliation on me. These people had given me a clear warning sign via their medicine man. I had understood their message.

Maybe the night bird was an owl. Sometime after that, and at a different place, I saw an owl in the storeroom of a medicine man; but that owl was dead. Even if that owl in the medicine man's storeroom was dead, at least that much can be said that an owl forms part of the paraphernalia of a medicine man. Maybe the night bird that was despatched to me was a different species of night bird. Because the shrieking of the night bird had been distorted by magical means, I was unable to identify its call as belonging to a bird species known to me.

Sending a bird as message is, compared to other messages that are also mainly nocturnal in nature and covered with a curse, a harmless affair. Despatching a night bird to someone is supposed to scare that person, which is also the main purpose of such an act. And, on top of that, the affected person is deprived of a couple of hours of sleep. If no other such acts follow the despatching of a night bird, the victim will suffer no further psychological or physical ill-effects.

Apart from an owl being despatched as a bird, there are other animals, too, that can be sent on a journey with the aim to cause fear and terror or as a foreboding to even greater harm. As far as I know, these animals are: baboon, snake, a small dog and a *tokoloshe*. The latter can also take the shape of a very tiny human being. Similar to a goblin, a *tokoloshe*, according to its origins, did not form part of the earlier belief system of the *Batswana*. It was introduced to the *Sotho/Tswana* tribes during the period of amalgamation of peoples, brought about by migrating mine workers from the *Nguni* tribes of Natal who moved into the Transvaal region (today the North West province of South Africa), and by the subsequent urbanisation that took place. Since that time the Batswana not only know about the *tokoloshe*, but are also very afraid of it.

In some tribes the tribal totem is also despatched as an instrument to announce an impending harm to be done to a neighbouring territory. In the case of the *Bahurutshe*, for instance, this might be a baboon. But there are tribes of whom it is not known whether they employ their totem for nocturnal surprise visits. I am not aware of such practises among the *Bakwena*,[9] for instance, whose totem is the crocodile, that any crocodile has ever been despatched to make a clandestine nocturnal appearance. When an animal has been bewitched by magical means and is subsequently despatched, it does not only appear outside. It is also capable of penetrating objects like walls, and of placing the soul in great distress. There are instances where the animal that has been despatched by the sorcerer will perform its task by entering through locked doors and windows, or by appearing as a menace in the dream of a sleeping person. The practise of magic has found a way by which it can break through all mate-

---

[9] *Kwena* denotes the crocodile. The tribe has adopted the name of its totem animal, which is not exclusively the case with all tribes.

rial and physical boundaries in order to be on a par with the spiritual substance, or to place the soul at risk and force it to surrender.

The despatches in which only animals are deployed by magical means, i.e. where the sorcerer does not use any additional resources, take place soundlessly. The magically controlled animals cause a disturbance in the victim's life and can even be seen with the naked eye, but cannot be heard. In my case I never saw the night bird, nor did I hear it making any moving sound. If the light from my torch chased the bird away, one would have thought that it would utter a frightened screech; the flap of its wings, the rustling of leaves or crackle of small twigs would have been audible in the stillness of the night. There was not a sound. The bird did not utter a sound while it was flying. It was only after it had perched again at a certain distance that it continued to utter its unnatural shrieks.

A critical reader or a natural scientist might take issue with my observations and remarks, saying that I acted too naively in my new surroundings. I was being drawn into the peripheries of magic. Since I had arrived in the country only a short while ago, I could not have been familiar with the calls of night birds. Critics and rationalists might even go as far as saying: Did the author actually hear something or was it some kind of hallucination? His experience might possibly have been only an imaginary manifestation, induced by anxieties and loneliness in culturally unfamiliar surroundings. I propose to put forward a different, opposing view.

G.M. *Setiloane* (1976:48-53), a theologian from the tribe of the *Batswana*, has identified four different types of magic: 1. Sorcery that emanates from the heart (*Boloi ba pelo*), 2. Sorcery that emanates from the mouth *(Boloi ba molomo)*, 3. Witchcraft of the night (*Boloi ba bosigo*), and 4. Witchcraft of the day *(Boloi ba motshegare).*

According to *Setiloane* the first two types are harmless. They are deployed within the community if a broken-down interpersonal relationship needs to be restored. The two other types constitute the more serious cases. These can however still carry the approval of the community.

The first two types, "sorcery that emanates from the heart", and "sorcery that emanates from the mouth" differ in one respect, namely that no notice is given of the first type. The victim does not know from whom the despatch has emanated. With the second type, "sorcery that emanates from the mouth", it is evident as to who it was that initiated the despatch. If an argument has taken place between two people, for instance, where the defeated person can or will not accept the reason as to why he should be disadvantaged, he will leave the other person with the words: "Just you wait and see what happens" (*o tla se bona*). This can lead to a typical case of "sorcery emanating from the mouth."

My first experience of such a deployment of magic can be attributed, not to the first, but to the second type identified by *Setiloane*, who summarises these first two types by saying: "... there are some activities described as boloi, which promote the re-establishment of order, and are, therefore, good."[10] According to *Setiloane*, his first two types of magic are not only to be tolerated but are also permitted, as they serve to restore the broken community. "In both forms the moloi is an agent of harmony."[11] We can assume that *Setiloane*, with this description, is encouraging the defeated person to consult a medicine man. The medicine man, described in this instance as being a sorcerer, must intervene on behalf of the defeated person by sending a clandestine message to the person who gained the advantage over the defeated person, to the effect that he has made a mistake. *Setiloane* thereby approves of magic in its traditional application by the medicine man. Magic is therefore appropriate, since its purpose is to restore harmony within the family or community after some misconduct or a transgression has occurred.

One can take issue with *Setiloane's* perception of this matter. Whoever goes for this "penny" must then also go for the "pound", i.e. if magic is condoned in this small way, the door is opened for all other magical practises as well. To subsequently distinguish between insignificant and more serious assaults becomes well-nigh impossible. Who could arrogate the competence to themselves to assess the different cases accurately, seeing that almost all of them are carried out clandestinely?

---

[10] *Setiloane*, G.M., The Image of God among the Sotho-Tswana. Rotterdam: AA Balkema, 1976, p. 49.

[11] Cf., p. 50.

Over and above a decision that is taken concerning an individual case, the targeted person and the relatives involved need to be taken into consideration. The person in question is not informed as to what awaits him or her. Targeted individuals are unable to defend themselves unless they also utilise the services of a medicine man with the help of their relatives, to retaliate, in secret, and with the same hostile and unknown magical force. What started out as an insignificant matter can then turn into a bitter struggle that may end in death and bloodshed. In view of the fact that the person who is at the receiving end of a sorcerous despatch must likewise be taken into consideration, Bosch writes: "What is good magic in the eyes of one person may be destructive magic in the eyes of another, who is at the receiving end, so to speak, of the magic of the first."[12]

Seeing that the utilisation of magic is a clandestine matter, it defies any kind of control. And if there exists no scrutiny of magical practises, one may also assume that their power is sought by those who had at first gained the upper hand, but who subsequently became the defeated party, the underdog.

The utilisation of magic consists, for the most part, of the appropriation of power. If someone should now happen to have attracted power by magical means, someone else will involuntarily be endangered. This other person will often not even suffer any ill-effects himself, but rather be rebuked in this indirect way. If this other person is an adult, it may happen that his or her child will suffer from a chronic affliction, like a continuously swollen leg, for instance. A medical doctor in town will attempt to make a diagnosis but will find neither a disease nor the cause thereof. The child is an innocent party. Maybe its parents insulted someone in the neighbourhood. Within the collective concept of social life, it is not necessarily the person who has caused the transgression who will suffer. The liability rests on everyone. That way its effectiveness is greatly increased.

To date there exists no authority that takes issue with or assesses the sorcerer in indigenous communities, or even prescribes to him what he may or may not do. He can do just about anything that people who come to him in secret ask him to do; he will then carry out their

---

[12] Bosch, p. 38-62.

request and set to his objective with imagination and knowledge of the sorcerous despatch.

Only the ancestors can possibly intervene. They are ranked in a hierarchically orientated religious system above humans, and also above the medicine man. They do however only intervene on rare occasions. The ancestors acknowledge the position of the sorcerer. They condone his magic. They make no distinction between small (harmless) and evil magic. What may initially be a harmless despatch can give rise to something much worse with the retaliation measures taken by the person concerned. It is not only a good friendship that might be broken. Families, too, can be torn apart and blood can flow. The entire conflict is implicitly acknowledged by the ancestors. This does not detract in any way from the belief in the ancestors.

I came to South Africa on the basis of another belief. I can understand the belief in the efficacy of the ancestors. I have encountered a number of people wo have told me of experiences with their deceased ancestors. Some of them served as my church elders, and were also good friends of mine. I can nevertheless not share their belief. I can also not accept that the so-called small assaults of sorcery are supposed to be a clandestinely sent benign message to serve as a warning to someone, or to rebuke him or her. I am not alone in this opinion. African Christians share my point of view that the respect shown to the ancestors in popular – and collective belief is based on continual delusion. It is for this reason that the ancestors remain a reality especially for those people who believe in them. Other Christians – and these are significantly more than the first group – share my view that the utilisation of magic should be eschewed altogether. The practise of magic takes place clandestinely. An impending magical despatch is no public matter. Neither can it be scrutinised or monitored.

With the above-mentioned case of the despatched night bird I would much rather have welcomed it – if indeed I had offended the traditional African community – if someone had come to me and told me that my behaviour was objectionable to certain people, and that I should not repeat certain actions in their company. In the event that this attempt to solve the problem did not constitute a possible option, namely that the missionary in a rural area could be approached concerning the matter of his transgression, this would still have left open the traditional way of lodging a complaint. This traditional way is taken via the council of the elders. If someone would have publicly lodged a complaint, a couple of council members would have been appointed vicariously for the local community to come and speak to me. I would also have preferred a telephone call or a letter rather than the clandestine nocturnal despatch of the anomalous night bird. This first example showed me that I could insult or offend the African culture with my European habits and ideas, and that I should reconsider the way I expected to live my life.

The second example, following below, deals with a direct encounter I had with an African from Malawi who made a conscious decision to practise sorcery. This man made a living by practising his craft. Compared to this sorcerer, an African medicine man is first and foremost a physician who tends to the sick, but who can succumb to the practise of magic if asked to do so.

2. The hitchhiker – a "witch doctor"

a) The example:

Fifteen years lie between the first and second example. During this time, many changes occurred in South African society. The face of evil had nevertheless hardly changed at all. It inflicted harm on other people in my immediate surroundings or further afield. Several cases were brought to my attention. I personally was not on the receiving end during this time. Then, one day, the following occurred: I was driving in my car, on my own, on one of the gravel roads in South Africa. Upon leaving the outskirts of a larger town I saw a number of hitchhikers standing next to the road.

I stopped, as I had done in all the previous years. A well-dressed young man of around 40 years of age climbed into the car. He seated himself next to me. We looked at each other. Slowly the car started moving forward. I greeted him in *Setswana*. He returned the greeting. I could tell by the way he greeted me that he was a foreigner. We had not even concluded our salutations when I began to experience pain in my abdominal region. The pain became more intense. The little Suzuki Minibus moved forward rather slowly. I put my head on the steering wheel. In order to bear up against the stabbing pain, I gripped the steering wheel tighter with my hands. My fellow passenger was sitting and observing me. Three times in succession he told me: "I am a witch doctor. I am a witch doctor. I am a witch doctor." If I held my breath I was able to contain the pain. When I breathed it became unbearable. For several minutes I only took short, sharp breaths. My fellow passenger and I remained silent for a long time. I felt anger rising towards this man. I asked myself: Why did he do this to me? Will he demand something of me to show me that he can humiliate me, or does he want to help me? I contemplated the matter and decided that I would under no circumstances ask him for his help. But neither did I want to boot the fellow from my car. After a while the pain became a little more bearable, and I struck up a conversation with him. My first question was: Do you carry harmful potions in your clothing? "No", came the reply. I believed him; he wore no jacket, carried no aspergillum, pouch or bag, neither did he wear a cap on his head, which is often worn to denote a medicine man. Do you have your divining bones in your trouser pocket? "No, I left my bones at home." Again I was obliged to believe him. His trouser pockets were empty. They lay flat against his legs. What did it signify that he had inflicted this pain on me, and by what means had he brought it about? Seeing that he was not particularly talkative I didn't want to ask him any more questions. He would probably have protested his innocence. I was unable to confront him with proof or facts of any kind.

We conducted our conversation in English. His proficiency in *Setswana*, the language spoken by the Africans in the then Transvaal and in which I attempted to have a conversation with him, did not extend beyond the words of salutation. This realisation prompted me to ask him questions of a more personal nature. I asked him where he came from. "I come from Malawi", he said. Why did you come to South Africa? "I go to wherever the people call me. I have already helped many people. White and black, Indian and coloured people, they all call me. There are many people in Botswana, Tanzania, Malawi and South Africa who know me." After about 30 minutes we parted company. My travelling companion gets out of the car in the vicinity of Sun City, while I turn right to continue on my journey. As he gets out, he takes his leave once again and hands me his calling card that bears the incomplete address: SAMUEL PAWANYIRENDA, SPECIAL STUDIO.

b) The explanation

The encounter with Mr Pawanyirenda was very odd indeed. I have had numerous encounters with local medicine men and women on the street, in homes and also in hospitals while paying someone a visit, and some have even visited me in my office as parishioners looking to ease their conscience. On one occasion, acting on an invitation extended to me by a medicine man whom I knew, I attended an annual meeting of around 200 medicine men and women, which took place roughly 100 km north of Pretoria, during the course of which I also sat down to eat with them. A great variety of herbs and a vast array of plant-based medicines were on display in a fairly large courtyard. Never before had any medicine man inflicted such pain on me, the effects of which I still felt three days later. Only on one occasion, during an informative visit to the store room of a famous local medicine man in *Bapong*, did I feel affected by an oppressive, sorcerously charged force, which was contained in the medicinal supplies and pervaded the entire store room. It was only after three days that I was totally able to shake off the disconcerting feeling that this force had elicited from me and that I am barely able to describe.

Mr Pawanyirenda had to have had something concealed in his clothing after all. Or else he had anointed himself with a very strong medicine to protect himself, which had had a very adverse effect on me? If either of these possibilities can be assumed to have been the case, why did I not pick up any strange or different, strong odour during our entire trip together? One thing is clear. A local medicine man would not have dared to plot such an assault on someone he is travelling with. A local medicine man who was well-known in his neighbourhood and region would have put his reputation and vocation at risk with an act like that. By whatever means Mr Pawanyirenda had carried out his assault, it could only be a foreigner who would dare to do that, someone who moved from one place to another, who was unable to produce a fixed abode with a consulting room, a man who would be long gone if someone should denounce and go after him.

After I had returned home I did not want to keep my experience from some of my trusted parishioners. Initially the men responded by laughing. Then they became more serious and said: "You have been taken in by a witch doctor who was looking to get some money from you." The motive may have been money. There are indeed numerous instances where it becomes apparent that the traditional medicine man, rather than following his initial vocation to heal people, succumbs to the temptation to mix his vocation with business.[13]

If the motive for the assault was indeed money, the question still remains as to how Mr Pawanyirenda went about executing it. The means to achieve his aim was not good, constructive medicine but rather of an evil, harmful kind. But how did he manage to transmit this harmful, pain-inducing medicine into my body? It is obvious that he must have planned his assault. He sees a European man sitting alone in his car who may be wealthy enough to pay for treatment, and who, in the event of any harm caused to him, will not be able to provide any proof of what has occurred. The European man stops and gives him a lift. There is no witness in the car who might be able to come to his aid and defend him. The number plate of the car indicates a region of origin further away. The other hitchhikers stood further back from the road. Pawanyirenda was the only one who stood up front. His chances were good. As he climbs into the car, and while he deems himself to be unobserved, he places the concealed medicine into his mouth. After he has settled into his seat he blows an odourless, sorcerously charged breeze into the direction of the driver. After the first inhalation the effect of his premeditated plan immediately takes hold.

---

[13] While gathering all kinds of examples of traditional spirit manifestations, an informant takes me to a medicine man. This medicine man told me of the following incident that occurred in an entirely different region: 'One night I was outside, tending to my business. A man I was familiar with approached me. I knew that he was planning to do something evil in one of the neighbouring houses. He was a sorcerer; I was a medicine man. I used my power to stop him. He had to turn around and go home. The next day he paid me a visit. He said: I know that you are stronger. You also have the power to kill me. But consider this: If you kill me, how will you make a living?' A short explanation: If the sorcerer causes someone to fall ill during the night, that person will go to the medicine man in the morning, asking for a cure. The treatment costs money.

Samuel Pawanyirenda introduced himself as 'witch doctor'. He is not a medicine man. The meaning of 'witch doctor' is that of sorcerer; the *Setswana* phrase is *'ngaka ya boloi'* ('doctor of sorcery/witchcraft'). The English word 'witch doctor' and the explanation in *Setswana 'ngaka ya baloi'* denote the same thing, whereas the English word 'sorcerer', even if not completely wrong, is however lacking in the basic meaning of the word. According to the original meaning of the word, a 'witch doctor' is a doctor who investigates acts of sorcery.

Originally the word 'witch doctor' denoted a doctor who dealt specifically with witchcraft, a meaning that is open to different interpretations. On the one hand – and this is the older version – there is the doctor who combats witchcraft. On the other, there is the doctor – examples of whom may be found in adequate numbers these days – who supplies the witches with the sorcerous medicines they require to perform their assaults, as the witches don't concoct these potions themselves. A collaboration between the two is therefore inevitable.

Pawanyirenda is not a medicine man who heals wounds, cures the sick and can foresee events that will take place tomorrow. He is also not one of those traditional medicine men who have received a calling to do the work they do. Those medicine men who follow an inner calling when they perform their work discern an illness by means of afflatus and visions imparted to them from the ancestral collective and administer the medicine pertaining to that illness, also via the ancestors. Pawanyirenda neither inherited nor acquired his occupation. He never received a calling. Neither did the ancestors force him to do what he does, as is often assumed in other cases. For instance, recurring bouts of fainting are often construed as being a form of ancestral intervention. He probably chose this occupation out of his own volition. He wanted to do this and opted to turn to sorcery.

If magical practises can be divided into black and white magic, or rather into witchcraft of the day or night, as G.M. *Setiloane*,[14] K. Koch,[15] as well as many other authors have done, or W. Janzen[16] who proffers

---

[14] Op. cit., p. 44.48.

[15] Op. cit., p. 125.

[16] Op. cit., p. 34.

to differentiate between "a receptive and an active method", then Pawanyirenda belongs to those who utilise black magic or witchcraft of the day. H.O. Mönnig[17] comments: "... witchcraft of the day is the learned ability to cast spells and use medicines to the detriment of others."[18]

The third case I am about to present deals with a series of negative spirit manifestations, paltering with me at night and setting upon me while I was asleep. The third example has a long prior history, to which I am merely able to allude. The parsonage had already previously experienced assaults from evil spirits before I moved in.

3. Sorcery and manifestations of witchcraft

a) The example:

Rumours began circulating that there was some kind of trouble in the parsonage. Nobody knew for certain what this trouble actually was. The ministry post for the congregation became vacant. When I received a telephone call – I resided in Germany at the time, furthering my studies in mission theology – inquiring whether I would be prepared to move to the township (settlement consisting exclusively of Africans) of *Ga-Rankuwa* with my family, I didn't give much thought to what possible unresolved trouble there could be in the parsonage. What captivated me much more was the prospect of working as a missionary in a congregation in a black suburb of Pretoria with around 100,000 inhabitants, and residing there as the only white family under what was still the Apartheid regime of South Africa in those days. The local superintendent told me later that the church council had asked whether he would be willing to accept a transfer to *Ga-Rankuwa*. He told me that he rejected the offer to be transferred. After I had ministered to the congregation for eight months, the reason for his refusal became clear to me. The house seemed to be haunted.

These spirit manifestations were a huge problem for my predecessor, a local pastor. He suffered greatly because of them and became seri-

---

[17] Op. cit., p. 71.

[18] Ibid.

ously ill. He would probably even have died if he hadn't hastily abandoned the property in the nick of time. The nature of the assault during these manifestations, as they occurred during his tenure, was always the same. The individual assaults, however, differed from one another. A manifestation initiated by sorcerous enactments has an arsenal of many different despatches at its disposal. My predecessor, a courageous pastor who firmly opposed traditional incidents informed by magical powers, was, due to his affinity to his own African culture, probably more prone to assaults from spirits than I, who was only familiar with hauntings of this kind in the German regions of the Lüneburg Heath, the North Sea coastline and the Black Forest through stories from an earlier age.

After the scare of the first manifestation I kept a diary of the events. These diary entries from 1984 to 1987 are as follows:

5 July: Thursday morning, 6 am. There is a knock on the door to the inner courtyard. I get up immediately and go to the door. There is nobody behind the door. I look around the courtyard. Nobody there either.

8 July: Around midnight. I wake up shortly after 1 am. I heard somebody knocking. Again three knocks on the door to the courtyard. I get up, go to the door. Nobody there.

7 September: It is 00:50 am. I am woken up again. This time three cautious yet clearly audible knocks on the same inner courtyard door. I don't get up, don't go to the door, neither do I go into the dark night outside.

11 January: I am rudely awakened at 1:12 am by three commanding, hard and rapid knocks on the door to the inner courtyard. I don't get up. I don't go to the door.

29 May: Around 00:52 am I hear a very hard, unusually loud bang. I am wide awake, but am unable to locate the apparent explosion. Did it come from the front or the back? I think it might have come from the back, i.e. from outside. The hostile bomb attacks of the Second World War spring to my mind; but the house is still standing. The window panes have not shattered. What has happened? A little while later the idea takes hold in my mind that something unnatural must

have happened in my head. A hostile force has made advances on my psyche and my consciousness.

As far as this incident is concerned I have to add that, immediately before this apparent explosion, two very unfamiliar, totally strange visions appeared to me. Each vision caused me to wake up. In the first vision the head of an antelope appears. I see the two sable horns more than anything else. Two snakes are coiling themselves upwards around the horns. In the second vision I see a black cat, standing with arched back and erect tail, somewhere in an open sandy space, maybe a Batswana homestead.

12 July: Shortly after 2 am I am awakened by a strange noise that I am not able to define.

12 August: I spend the night with friends on a mission station in the Western Transvaal, 250 km away from Ga-Rankuwa. During the night, two men appear to me in a dream vision. The men are approaching from the direction of the nearby cemetery. One of them stands head and shoulders above the other. The two men are wearing black clothes. They walk past the church down the hill towards the parsonage. They come to a halt in front of the window of the guest room where I am sleeping. Then I hear a loud bang, which is however not as forceful as the strange explosion at Ga-Rankuwa. I wake up and look out the window. The moon is shining. Nobody to be seen.

12 October: I am working in the evening. I only go to bed after midnight. After having slept for only a short while, I am woken at around 2 am by a gentle substance stroking my face. I sit up in my bed. In front of me, to the right, I see a veil or a scarf, broad at the bottom and tapering towards the top, where it appears to be rather more hazy. The shape is rising from the bed, moving up towards the ceiling. The shadowy form looks like a cloak, a long dress or a night gown. The nebulous veil shape floats further upwards over my wife's bed. The shape dissolves between the bedroom ceiling and the outside wall and disappears from the room. My wife, who is sleeping next to me, did not notice a thing.

23 February of the following year: At around 1:30 am something wakes me. A violent, unusually loud and diabolical rattling noise is emanating from the street behind our house. My first thought is that

an army tank has gone astray in our area. Later I compared the sound of the vehicle to that of a motorcycle that belongs to someone in the neighbourhood. The further away the persistent noise moves, the louder and more demonic it sounds. Then it seems as if the vehicle turns into a northerly direction. The sound slowly fades to finally disappear altogether.

11 October of the following year: At around 4:45 am I wake up. The room is pervaded by a strong smell of freshly cooked meat, the way the Batswana cook it in three-legged iron pots at large festivals, for instance. One window stands ajar. I am too tired to get up and to go through the house or even outside. Soon I am asleep again. When I get up an hour later, the smell has left the room.

17 October of the following year: At 8:30 pm our then five-year-old son, after returning to his bedroom from the toilet and having seen something in the kitchen, says to me: "Father, I just saw a very tall man. He was in the kitchen, walking from the cupboard over to the kitchen sink. He was wearing big black shoes. He wore a black garment. Father, I'm scared that the man will come into our bedroom."

23 January of another year, a couple of weeks before our transfer to Brits: I am woken by two soft knocks on the side wall against which my bed stands. It is 5:55 am. There is no bed on the other side of the wall.

b) The explanation

I ministered to the congregation in *Ga-Rankuwa* for three years and three months. For a pastor that is not a very long time. According to the records at hand, manifestations of supernatural powers occurred twelve times during this period. In two-and-a-half years, twelve incidents of hauntings occurred.[19]

---

[19] I am able to refer to those manifestations at *Ga-Rankuwa* as hauntings (German: *Spuk,* Afrikaans: *spook*). I refer to hauntings as being all those experiences which a human mind, intellect or will can produce during its lifetime by way of magical teachings and clandestine implementation, or else as an apparition after a person's death; these experiences are brought about by supernatural means, insinuated into nature, thereby frightening people by abusing, animating, displacing and dis-

On average, the manifestation of hostile powers occurred once every ten weeks, or four to five times a year. Not one of these disturbances happened during the day. One occurred in the evening, two in the early morning, all the others around midnight. It may ostensibly be stated that the disturbances occurred after dark. However, a specific order can as yet not be established from the manifestations.

If we look at the days, weeks and months, we can ascertain that the spirits have no preference for a specific month, week or day. They make one appearance in January in two different years, once only in February; not at all in March, April and June, once in May. They manifest once in July in two different years, once in August; once in September, three times in October in two different years; not at all in November and December.

The time of year apparently plays no part. The spirits appear both in summer as well as winter.[20] Also, they skip a few summer and winter months.

The spirits seem not to be particularly interested in the different seasons. The same can be said about weekdays. The spirits have no interest in a particular day of the week. Something else becomes apparent, however. The intention of their appearance is geared towards the object. They do not appear on Tuesday and Wednesday nights. They only appear once on a Thursday. On each of the Saturdays, Sundays and Mondays they appear twice, and five times on a Friday. The focal point of their appearances is obviously on Fridays, as well as the days following Fridays, i.e. Saturday, Sunday and Monday. Those are the weekend days. And, besides these weekend days, the nights on either side of them. The spirits make an appearance exactly at those times when the church is in demand and the missionary is urgently in need of a good night's sleep.[21]

---

torting God's creation, or else by extravagant fraudulent deceptions that seem to be real, natural and constructive.

[20] The seasons in South Africa are the exact opposite of those in the northern hemisphere.

[21] One may admittedly ponder on the psychological explanation that the missionary did somehow not cope with the psychological strain placed on him by his workload, especially over weekends, and that this circumstance prompted these appari-

It is strange that I did not record a single incident during the first eight months. This must be of significance. Only after eight months does the first disturbance occur, and is subsequently repeated on numerous occasions. During the following six months an apparent knocking occurs four times, always the same knocking, always the same door. One can understand that I initially assume that somebody is there, standing behind the door, seeking help. After I see through this deception I show no interest anymore. The occult power then seeks to provoke me. With the fourth knocking, it replies with thunderous bangs onto the same door, thereby indicating an escalation of its efforts. It then suspends its treacherous knocking for a long period of time.

It soon comes up with another way to intensify its assaults. For a couple of minutes during the night of the 29th of May I have no idea what is going on around me. The same assault occurs once more in a slightly different and attenuated form, when I stay overnight elsewhere. In both instances the sequence of events is the same. The spirit power inserts one, or rather two visions before each of the unusual bangs. I had never had such visions up to that point. The unfamiliar visions were part of the agenda of that hostile force. Their aim was to put the targeted person into a state of twilight sleep so that the actual assault following after the visions would be all the more frightening in its effect.

The images in the visions vary in content. The two images in the first vision bear the same message. In European and Christian society, both the snake and the black cat symbolise something negative and evil. The snake symbolises sin. And, since the Middle Ages, the black cat came to be a symbol for the devil.

---

tions to manifest in his subconscious mind, or even the more banal explanation that the church has always been concerned with the devil; these explanations do however not apply, for the following two reasons: firstly, it wasn't because of me that the *Ga-Rankuwa* hauntings made an appearance in the parsonage. Several of my predecessors reported similar occurrences. Especially my immediate predecessor had been severely affected by them. Secondly, that was the first time something like that happened to me, even though I had been in the ministry for a number of years by then.

In the second vision two men appear, all dressed in black. The power behind the scenes lets them rise from their graves. Their black attire represents the intervention of death, something this power expedites and desires. This image is supposed to frighten and unsettle the missionary.

One has to interpret the images in these visions in connection with the assaults themselves. While the assaults represent a very real hostile power, the images are a symbolic expression, a manifestation of the existence of that power.

Some of those twelve manifestations repeat themselves while others remain isolated incidents. The knocking spirit is heard several times, making altogether five appearances, pointing towards the preferred modus operandi of that particular spirit power. The apparent explosions are repeated twice. That the spirit power makes use of knocking is understandable insofar as it has, by doing so, established a direct connecting factor. During the day, many people come and knock on the door of the missionary's office. The spirit power has now simply transferred this daytime occurrence into the night.

The so-called explosions, as well as the rattling noise with diabolical overtones are an expression of strength and power. They were deployed to serve as intensification. The objective is to force the missionary into surrender. The diabolically sounding rattling noise and the knocking warrant similar observations. Both are transformations. However, they differ in the sense that the knocking spirit takes up a common daily occurrence and transformed it into the night, whereas the diabolical rattling is transformed by way of adoption. A motorcycle drives past the missionary's house in the middle of the night. The spirit power seizes this opportunity. It adopts the engine sound, multiplies and amplifies its frequency and aims it at its object.

On one occasion, on the 12th of July, I am woken shortly after 2 am by a strange noise. I cannot compare this noise to anything else. It sounded neither like a twig that brushes across the roof in the wind, nor like the nocturnal activities of a cat, mouse or rat, nor like any sound that could have been made by a human being or an electrical household appliance during the night. This sound might also have been a transformation, a supposition that cannot be verified in this case; it may however possibly have been derived from a remnant of one of the previous spirit manifestations.

It is a common occurrence that spirit manifestations are accompanied by noise. Everyday – as well as unusual noises are part of a spirit's arsenal. F. Moser calls this kind of manifestation "mimicry noises".[22] Mimicry noises are something that is adopted to imitate human or animal noises, as well as something that is repeated in the manifestation from a previous historical event or occurrence. Mimicry noises cannot be interpreted or explained by normal organs of perception. They are understood as being a retention of events that occurred sometime in the past and have subsequently attached themselves to the scene of that event. That is where they slumber. They can be awakened when certain situations arise. As 'physical traces' they are a residue of times gone by. Moser describes these mimicry noises in such a way that an investigation into them will not yield a conclusive result.

On the basis of the events presented above, as well as additional examples compiled by me, the mimicry noises mentioned by Moser are rated by the *Batswana* people as forming a part of sorcerous assaults of magic. I deduce this assertion from the context of individual cases in which similar noises occurred alongside other manifestations, as was the case with the assaults in *Ga-Rankuwa*. The haunting quality of the mimicry noises does, in that case, not constitute an autonomous or objective form of manifestation. It signifies a manifestation – among other possible forms – of manipulations set in motion by the spirit force. It does however appear to be possible that the so-called mimicry noises can be bound in a more powerful way to the targeted site where the spirit manifestations are to be deployed, and will continue to have an effect even after other forms of manifestations from the same apparition have already been banished or dispelled. I have no doubt in my mind that they were initiated by the sorcerers of the Batswana people.

The indefinable noise I heard in *Ga-Rankuwa* actually occurred after what is commonly known as the witching hour around midnight. Another focal point that can be attributed to half the number of mani-

---

[22] Op. cit., p. 534.

festations at *Ga-Rankuwa* is that they occurred during the two hours after midnight, i.e. midnight to 2 am. Spirits appear more frequently at midnight than at any other times of the day or night. Spirit sorcery places its focus on midnight. And midnight during full moon is even more conducive to magic. The earth and moon have their own laws during that time, something the sorcerer probably views in an opportune light.

In connection with the spirits around midnight, I am reminded of stories that our teachers read to us on the last day of school before the holidays started, after our reports had already been written: They told us of witches who, skittering at breakneck speed across villages and forests at midnight, head for the Brocken in the Harz mountains, coming from all over and gathering there to feast, exchange experiences and making plans for their next get-together. When D. Irvine was crowned queen of the witches for one year, she met up with her princesses at midnight for the witches' dance at Exmoor in Britain.[23] I will revisit the topic of witches and their manifestations at a later stage.

As far as such manifestations occur among the *Batswana*, one has to take their traditional belief into account which holds that, at midnight and also at noon when the sun is at its zenith, the ancestors are resting. This means that they will not intervene at those times. Taking this understanding into consideration as well, the time around midnight or high noon is more favourable for a sorcerer or witch doctor to launch his assault. The ancestors don't see or notice much during this time. Therefore they will also not be able to overrule an evil deed. A human's shadow is presented as outward sign in this regard, which is thought to signify the ancestral soul that accompanies one. Seeing that one's shadow is shorter at noon on a sunny day or during a moonlit night at midnight, the human body is less protected at those times.

Sorcerous acts and spirits are not bound to midnight to be effective, however. This is borne out by the manifestations at *Ga-Rankuwa* and many other events involving spirits that took place during the day. The appearance of a ghost person can be seen as some sort of cul-

---

[23] Op. cit., p. 100.

mination at *Ga-Rankuwa*. Our son walks down the passage to his bedroom. While doing so, his attention is caught by a strange event that is happening in the kitchen. The kitchen door is wide open. An apparition of a figure appears in the kitchen. The boy is startled. I calm him down. I also experience a certain degree of unease. Then it occurs to me that I am not the person who chose this house to live in. In the name of the Lord who sent me I proceed to search all the rooms. The result: There is no trace of any person in our house that was locked up at the time.[24]

Following on the *Ga-Rankuwa* cases related above, we are able to ascertain a further interim finding. The spirits started out fairly harmlessly. Their first manifestations were of a tolerable nature. The knocking increased in intensity, however, when the targeted person showed some resistance. The resistance persisted. The spirits modify their assaults. They deploy harsher measures that can probably be traced back to some form of technology. The so-called bomb attacks or the terrifying rattling noises are yet again supposed to be a special demonstration of their inexhaustible powers. When this also fails to produce the desired result and the assaulted person is still offering resistance, the situation culminates with the projection of a person into the scene by way of a haunted ghost. Prior to the apparition in the form of an imaginary person, the spirits had come up with something else. It was no longer enough for them to be involved with only one adversary. Their attacks are broadened to include other members of the immediate family. My wife, who was sleeping next to me, never heard a thing of this entire deception. Our oldest son as well as

---

[24] At a later time, while reading Martin Luther's ghost stories, I stumbled upon something similar. In one of his numerous devil stories, Luther also invokes his mission in a conversation with the devil. He writes: "The devil has often raised a racket in the house and has tried to scare me, but I appealed to my calling and said: 'I know that God has placed me into this house to be lord here. Now if you have a call that is stronger than mine and are lord here, then stay where you are. But I well know that you are not lord here and that you belong in a different place – down in hell.' And so I fell asleep again and let him be angry, for I well knew that he could do nothing to me." Walch Vol. III, p. 1915. (Official English translation of Luther text)

our daughter never experienced any disturbance. But our second son is drawn into the events.[25]

It is unlikely that our five-year-old son conjured up this ghostly person from his imagination. Rather, it was brought to his attention. There were specific reasons as to why the spirit power, in its manifestation as a ghostly figure, elected to approach the child, thereby involving the rest of the family in its messages of terror.

There are many instances of sorcery and hauntings by evil spirits involving children. My observations in this regard are as follows: If sorcery in Africa is, for whatever reason, aimed at a specific family, it is in many cases an innocent child that is targeted first by making it ill. However, if a spirit apparition and hauntings are the result of this sorcery, a child will only be involved in the events at a later stage.[26]

The assumption can be made that the reason why the spirits are drawn to a child in their ghost person manifestations may be found in the fact that the mind of a child has not yet reached that phase of its life where it questions and challenges everything; its childlike faith is therefore more receptive to an apparition.

The *Ga-Rankuwa* cases covered so far are all attributable to sorcery. It is a sorcerous act that has been initiated. The sorcerer himself is not aware of the detailed aspects of an assault and the extent of its impact. All kinds of spirit manifestations, being the result of initiated assaults, have their origin in the spirit power. The sorcerer has tapped into the spirit power with his knowledge, and with a specific objective in mind. The spirit power has subsequently carried out the so-called request in its own way. As long as sorcery remains a feature in Africa the various stories of hauntings and spirit manifestations, introjected by tapping into and the use of magic, will continue to surface.

Of the manifestations that occurred in *Ga-Rankuwa*, there are two examples that have not been dealt with during the analysis so far.

---

[25] Our children, aged three, five and seven years at the time, knew nothing of the hauntings that were going on. We had neither television nor any books about ghost stories. Klaus was a healthy boy.

[26] This also becomes apparent in movies such as 'Poltergeist' I and II.

There is a specific reason for that. They fall into a different category of sorcery. The incidents in question are those that occurred on 12 October and 11 October of the following year. I cannot say as to whether the month of October is immaterial in this regard or not. We may assume that those two manifestations both happened in October by coincidence. In the first instance a seemingly moving, nebulous mass or figure appears in the main bedroom. I didn't see any figure or shape in the second instance. I am roused from a deep sleep by a strong, familiar smell of cooked meat. Both instances originate from the same source. How is one able to discern this? What do they have in common? What sets them apart from the other manifestations? These two manifestations have been executed by witches.

Sorcerers and witches work collaboratively with one another. Witches can also perform various things on their own. But in many cases they have to rely on the sorcerer for help. In the two instances above, a witch has obviously been at work. The witch, a normal person by day and a church-goer on Sundays, is upset about certain things that happened in the congregation. Maybe she has also been accused of not having exercised one of the congregational responsibilities assigned to her. She feels aggrieved. She then proceeds, in her own way and possibly together with others who know her and her business, to bring about some form of retaliation.[27]

Originally the activity of witches and sorcerers was, for the most part, geared towards their own extended family. These lines were crossed in instances where quarrel and jealousy had spread into the wider neighbourhood. The old order of affiliation along extended family lines is no longer in place. In the cities it is the congregation that, to a large extent, assumes the role of the extended family and the neighbourhood. This led to the circumstance that the still-existent witches have shifted their field of operation to the new community and its surroundings. Once witches have set their minds on something, they will not hesitate to operate within the Christian congregation too.

---

[27] During ancient times, witches were almost exclusively women who took on a subordinate role towards men in their traditional communities. Batswana society is undergoing a change, however, which has led to the fact that men, too, can operate as witches or rather sorcerers (warlocks) in today's society.

Three different characteristics point to the fact that a witch was at work in *Ga-Rankuwa*. Witches are known to only gather at their arranged meeting place very late at night. It is also known that they only leave their gathering well after midnight, sometimes only in the early morning hours. It is a known fact that witches take their lead from sorcerers. When sorcerers execute an assault, witches do not plan theirs during the same time. In *Ga-Rankuwa*, the witch appeared once at 2 am and, on the other occasion, at 4:45 am in the early morning. It cannot be excluded that she paid frequent visits on other occasions as well, but she was not conspicuous on those occasions.[28] Firstly, one is able to recognise her because of the time when she appears. While the ten instances of sorcery were conducted between 8:30 pm to 6 am with focal times in the evening, around midnight and in the morning, the witch conducts her business between midnight and morning. In both instances it may be assumed that a witch paid the parsonage a visit after having returned from a witch feast or gathering, having executed an assault via the sorcerer, or else that she is connected to the assault through her circle of acquaintances and that she established sympathies towards the sorcerous assaults that were orchestrated. She herself only appears on the scene for a visit. Secondly, she could be discerned as being a witch by her nebulous garment, which appeared to be wide at the bottom and tapering towards the top. A sorcerer (warlock) would probably have opted for a different guise. During her second appearance the witch cannot be seen, only detected by smell. The smell suggests that she not only attended a gathering of witches, but that she was also attending a feast during which freshly cooked meat was served. The witch feast lasted till the early hours of the morning.

Witches have all but disappeared from public life in Germany, and Europe in general. The era of brutal witch hunts during the late Middle Ages is gone for good. But witches do nevertheless still exist.

---

[28] Mention should be made of one exception: During a visit from my parents-in-law, we made our bedroom available to them. The following morning, while having our coffee, my father-in-law said: 'Strange things happen in your house at night. Is the place haunted?' He spoke vehemently as he had slept very poorly. He was about to tell us what happened, but my wife interrupted him and the conversation turned to other things.

They hold their covens, turn night into day, utilise magic for their own purposes, seek advice from demons and spirits, exact malicious vengeance on people who have insulted them, join the church of Satan, etc.

O. Schnurr[29] quotes an interview with Petra S., a witch, in a German edition of the Cosmopolitan magazine[30]. The interview quotes the following important information, pertaining also to the witches among the *Batswana*; Petra S. states: "I get up when it suits me, usually between eleven in the morning and five in the afternoon ... At night I often meet up with other witches and sorcerers."[31] These statements about a witch's concept of time are in step with the nocturnal visits of the witch in *Ga-Rankuwa*. If a witch goes about her normal life during the day or likes to sleep in now and again, she will not necessarily be distinguishable from other people.

Petra goes on to say: "I live my life. Very peacefully. But if someone harms or wrongs me, I get incredibly angry. I take measures to really hurt that person. I avenge myself."[32] When Petra S. intends to exact vengeance on a person, she constantly thinks of that person until something nasty has happened to him or her. She says: "I take revenge ... by concentrating extremely hard on that particular person. I picture a scene where something happens to this person, for example. And then I keep on visualising this image. I constantly think of it until 'it' finally happens."[33] As straightforward, dangerous but also imperious and wrathful as it sounds, it becomes nonetheless clear that thoughts are not merely wind, smoke and mirrors, but are able to transfer power onto others, causing the soul to experience severe

---

[29] Op. cit., p. 60-66.

[30] 10/1985, p. 32-33.

[31] 'Ich stehe auf, wann es mir passt, meistens zwischen elf Uhr vormittags und fünf Uhr nachmittags ... Nachts treffe ich oft andere Hexer und Hexen.'

[32] 'Ich lebe mein Leben. Ganz ruhig. Aber tut mir jemand etwas an, werde ich unheimlich sauer. Ich ergreife Maßnahmen, damit es demjenigen schlecht ergeht. Ich räche mich.'

[33] 'Ich räche mich ... indem ich mich wahnsinnig stark auf die betreffende Person konzentriere. Ich male mir eine Szene aus, wie dieser Person zum Beispiel etwas zustößt. Und dieses Bild halte ich mir ununterbrochen vor Augen. Ich denke ständig daran bis 'es' dann passiert.'

distress. A witch is often in possession of a strong will, as is the case with Petra S. She is also knowledgeable about herbs and roots that have the ability to heal or harm; she utilises these to bring about her assaults. She is also able to seek the advice of spirits for her endeavour. With the *Batswana*, these spirits are the ancestors from their own tribe. In a European context, however, this can be any spirit masquerading as a human being who lived hundreds of years ago.

Petra S. has the following to say about the nocturnal meetings and the witches' excursions or visits to various places during which they take on a different guise or transform into a translucent mass: "Only the astral body (is present). You cover yourself in flying ointment from the waist to the neck, and then you exit your body. Only a thin thread remains to connect you (to your body). You can slip into flowers, trees, or other people. You feel really wonderful during all of this."[34] As easy as it sounds, that "slipping into" remains as incomprehensible and inexplicable to an ordinary person.

Petra S. is not alone in her depictions. D. Irvine didn't have the time to cover herself in flying ointment. She, together with her fellow trevellers, were suddenly caught off guard at midnight by an evangelist and two journalists who were looking for witches that night. Irvine, who found her way back to normal life and who experienced a long protracted conversion and had to muster great resistance against the forces of evil that continued to beset her, states in her autobiography

---

[34] 'Nur der Astralkörper (ist anwesend). Man reibt sich mit Hexensalbe von der Taille bis zum Hals rauf ein, und dann geht man raus aus dem Körper. Es bleibt nur noch ein ganz dünner Faden als Verbindung übrig. Man kann in Blumen, in Bäume, auch in Menschen hineinschlüpfen. Man hat ein total schönes Gefühl dabei.' – Among the *Batswana*, certain instances involving witches who have slipped into their own domestic animals or those of their neighbours have become well-known. The following two incidents were told to me first-hand: When a donkey and a pig were beaten in order for them to leave the front yard, a voice emanated from the animals, saying: 'Why are you beating me? It is hurting me.' Another case which resulted in legal proceedings occurred after a witch had slipped into a dog. One night, the dog was howling incessantly in front of a neighbour's door. As a consequence, the animal was brutally beaten by the home owner. It ran away. Its bloody trail led to the neighbour, in whose house a woman became seriously ill the following day for no apparent reason, succumbing to her illness a short while later.

"From Witchcraft to Christ": "I called up powers of darkness … Within seconds a green swirling mist enveloped us … My magic had worked. … The other witches and I were invisible to the three men, who were not even aware of the thick swirling mist. They had not seen a single thing."[35] D. Irvine also describes the arrival of witches at a coven: "Black witches from all parts of England assembled, as well as witches from Holland, Germany and France … They arrived in smart cars, not on broomsticks, and booked in at hotels looking for all the world like successful businessmen and women – which some were."[36]

Petra S. and D. Irvine possessed the power to transform themselves and become invisible to other people. Would the witch at *Ga-Rankuwa* not have had the same powers? If we can assume that witches have, in some instances, inherited the ability to transform themselves while having acquired this craft by submitting themselves to occult powers and sorcery in other instances, then the observation that witches are able to penetrate through matter and disappear should also not be dismissed out of hand. In Ga-Rankuwa the witch was seen in the main bedroom. She departed by moving off between the ceiling of the room and the outside wall. If this observation was indeed correct, it may be assumed that a witch is capable, by being in possession of magical powers, of transforming herself into a mass that is able to penetrate visible matter.

Sorcery has embarked on a similar path as witchcraft, which enables it to achieve similar things. Both utilise magic. However, whereas a sorcerer will only on very rare occasions insert his own person in a magical despatch and will rather only execute said despatch, namely that foreign matter will penetrate matter or will enter into other matter, a witch will perform her despatches in such a way that she can insert herself into the transformation process. Both methods employ magic which enables the person intent on presenting power in various ways to penetrate matter. B. Wenisch expresses this as follows: It has been observed "that, by all appearances, matter is able to penetrate matter, under the influence of psycho-kinetic energies,

---

[35] Op. cit., p. 100.

[36] Op. cit., p. 101.

to wit, that emanate from the elicitor of the haunting or rather are deployed by him or her."[37]

Witches undoubtedly operate autonomously with regard to other supernatural powers. As far as the Batswana are concerned, they perform various actions independently from the medicine man. They are nevertheless not autonomous in many other respects, or they seek connections to other powers or more powerful persons due to their own limitations. In the domain of the *Batswana* the witch calls on the medicine man, who will then collaborate with her in executing a certain matter, or else she will request of him to mandate her objectives and assaults. From the realm of spirits, she needs the consent of the ancestors who will only object to her clandestine undertakings on very rare occasions. In some cases, if the witch's strength and will are on the decline, this can lead to the circumstance that her own conscience will prick her. One of my informants told me about an old *Batswana* woman: "On several occasions I heard that woman talk about her scandalous deeds. She talks in a loud voice, and always just to herself; but she never talks about it when someone sees her or comes into close proximity of her."

During a conference held for theologians as well as laity at the University of Pretoria, a South African ballet teacher named McCord related her experience with the magical powers of witch craft and how she dealt with them. During a subsequent interview with the magazine *Huisgenoot*, dated 17 July 1986, she states: "I was a pretty witch who sang in the choir, was a Sunday School teacher and an active member of the church. A witch occupies a certain position in the church of Satan."[38] Satanic churches have not been in existence since ancient times, but they do follow a certain trend. In her book D. Irvine, too, who was a Bride of Satan for a year, describes a worship service of the Satanic Church of London.

One may infer from the examples listed above that evil has always been something that is sought out and initiated by humans. Two

---

[37] Op. cit., p. 88. – '...dass Materie allem Anschein nach Materie durchdringen kann, und zwar unter dem Einfluss psychokinetischer Energien, die vom Spukauslöser ausgehen bzw. von ihm eingesetzt werden.'

[38] *'Ek was 'n mooi heks wat in die koor gesing, Sondagskool gehou en aktief aan die kerklewe deelgeneem het. 'n Heks is 'n rang in die kerk van Satan, ...'*

ways of effecting this may be discerned. One way is that of the sorcerer. A request to initiate an evil deed is brought to him during a secret rendezvous. And, by sorcerous means, he finds a way of executing it. The other way of effecting evil assaults is through witchcraft. However, one needs to differentiate between at least two kinds of witchcraft that have become known to occur. One kind is known to the witch alone. It is the way by which a witch or warlock is able to turn themselves into a mass that is invisible to the human eye, or to slip into another being. This kind of witchcraft is easily recognisable as it serves only to frighten. The observer will not detect anything evil about it. Witchcraft only becomes evil when it sets in motion evil intent based on the witch's skills. This witchcraft will harm individual people but also the entire community.

Over and above the natural forces of the earth, as well as the beneficial and harmful energies of plants, sorcery and witchcraft seeks to hedge itself by means of the supernatural powers of the spirit world. In the case of the Batswana, these spirits are the ancestors that are summoned by deploying mediumistic, power- and magic-laden objects. The ancestors for their part can also intervene from the spirit world in an earthly event; but they don't do this very often. The spirit world is not always fundamentally evil in nature. It can allow evil to take place if this is what the sorcerer or witch desires. It is however also able to initiate an evil deed of its own accord.

In the spirit world there exist good and evil spirits. Ancestral spirits are good spirits, while evil spirits are those that have, for reason of some or other discontentment, not reached the spirit world of the ancestors. The ancestors play an important role among the *Batswana*. They are still taken into consideration even if there are individuals with secret malicious intent.

There was evil intent behind the assaults of *Ga-Rankuwa*. This evil intent is aimed at an opponent. The aim was to force the assaulted opponent into capitulation by causing him suffering. Practical magic was employed to attain this aim. Somebody initiated a process via the medicine man. The magical forces granted the request. They cleared the way for the spirit apparitions. The apparitions appear; there are many different magical possibilities to summon the spirits. But the assaulted person himself is not aware of the magical forces behind the spirits. He initially sees only the spirits. He is roused from his sleep and gets a fright. This sleep interruption has an impact on his soul as well; it becomes unsettled. It is being affected and challenged by an ungodly power. The harmonious entity of mind, body and soul begins to unravel. The soul begins to have doubts. Things that, up to that point, had been familiar and valuable to it become worthless all of a sudden, are put into different perspective, become pointless and possibly even meaningless. The missionary's faith, too, is strongly affected. For a while, he experiences such a spiritual crisis that he wants to abandon his inquiry into the spirit apparitions and change his occupation. More mention will be made of that later.

A further example that involves evil spiritual powers is the death of a young boy.

4. *Rrapula's* death

a) The example:

In the following example we meet the spirit power, that is to say a power makes an appearance that can be viewed as being an autonomous quantity. In the case of *Ga-Rankuwa* it has hitherto only appeared indirectly through the apparitions. It released and despatched the apparitions but, up to that point, it could not be discerned as being the initiator of these despatches. The spirit power executed the despatches in *Ga-Rankuwa* after it received the request to do so. It could not be discerned in a direct way, even though it acted as mediator in its own interests. It welcomed the request to release the spirits.

But now, in this context, it seeks an opportunity to present itself. It is afforded this opportunity. The spirit power contributes its part. The example *"Rrapula"* has to be connected to the incidents at *Ga-Rankuwa*. It happened at a time when the apparitions at *Ga-Rankuwa* came to a head. On 12 July 1986, at 7:30 pm, *Rrapula* commits suicide.

b) The explanation:

Rrapula is a 14-year-old boy. He is to be confirmed in the church in a few months' time. During confirmation classes he asks a number of serious questions. He is doing well in school. At home his mother devotes more time to him than to his older siblings.

According to *Setswana* custom the youngest son will inherit the house – the realm of the mother – and is obliged to look after her for the rest of her life. *Rrapula's* mother falls pregnant again with the child of another man. Just before the birth of the illegitimate child, *Rrapula* departs this life by hanging himself.

There is political unrest in *Ga-Rankuwa*, the aim of which is to bring about the downfall of Apartheid. 10 years after the *Soweto* uprising the unrest has spread to all black settlements. In *Ga-Rankuwa* people are killed and wounded. The opposition violently hauls young people out of their homes to co-opt them for their revolutionary campaigns, assaults and boycotts. In the evenings the youths run through the streets in large groups. The police beat them brutally and arrest many of them. The unrests might have been the reason for his suicide. *Rrapula* hates the police beatings and prison. He also hates the drugs that are distributed among the young people to act as stimulant for the revolutionary campaigns in the evenings.

Drugs could possibly have been a critical contributing factor why he ended his life in such untimely fashion. At least that is what many people suspected. However, a further reason which can be afforded greater weight needs to be taken into consideration. As the youngest child and future heir *Rrapula* had been given special attention by his mother. She particularly liked playing with him. The arrival of a newborn child puts an end to this kind of attention. He not only loses his inheritance but also that special motherly love. When all this becomes apparent to him he departs this life. At the time of Rrapula's suicide the previously mentioned conference took place in Pretoria. The topic of the conference was: "The Bible, the Church and Demonic Powers."

It is not only High German that is spoken in my home town in Germany, but also Low German. And in Low German we have a saying that picks up on the concomitant circumstances of that conference. It says: "If you speak of the devil he is already close by."[39] It was at that conference, where presentations were given on demonic powers,

---

[39] *'Wenn man vun 'n Dübel snackt, is he nich wiet.'*

that I felt someone slapping me from behind on my right shoulder.[40] Someone wanting to greet me? Did someone want to ask me something? On one side next to me sat a *Batswana* pastor. He was looking at the speaker. Another friend sat on my left side. He was busy writing. We were sitting on one of the last rows of seats in the lecture hall. Nobody sat behind us. I nonetheless looked behind me, but nobody was there. The time was 7:10 pm. The following morning, I was called out of the lecture hall. I was told about *Rrapula's* death.

The connections that exist between the incident in Pretoria and those at *Ga-Rankuwa* are striking. In Pretoria, lectures and talks are held on evil forces. Evil presents itself in a vast number of forms. While it presented itself in *Ga-Rankuwa* in disguised audible form, by way of visions, through smell and in human form, it manifests in Pretoria by way of physical touch. It does not touch the inner side of its opponent i.e. the soul, but rather his outer side, his body. Just like the evil force had, on a previous occasion, sought out its target in a desolate region,[41] so it repeats the assault on this occasion, too, outside its actual location of attack. It is not bound to local barriers in any way. It appears how and where it wants to. In doing so, it continues to deploy its imperious interference and disruption, only it does so by touching on this occasion. It wants the missionary to give up his resistance. And it will no longer suffice to only harass him in his own home with his family. The evil spirits will also not leave him in peace while he is attending a conference with his friends.

However, one may assume that, in Pretoria, a different magical force is at work as the one deployed in Ga-Rankuwa, where the spirit arsenal had been tapped into by a medicine man. In Pretoria the spirit force itself takes action. In view of the propounded talks that are held at such presentations on the subject of occultism, as well as the

---

[40] Medical doctors and psychologists could probably offer the explanation that this was a nervous twitch, brought on by some kind of fright. They surmise that, while listening to a presentation about demonic powers, the affected person is confronted with a problem that poses an as yet unresolved issue to him or her. That might have been the case if this had been an isolated incident unrelated to anything else. This is however only a preliminary answer. If one ties this incident in with those that happened at *Ga-Rankuwa,* the example takes on a different meaning.

[41] Cf. p. 28, journal entry dated 12 August.

theoretical and practical examples that were discussed pertaining to Satanism or demon possession, it is possible that the spirit power lay in wait. It was present, so to speak. It suited it well that the missionary was traumatised by the manifestations that had presented themselves at Ga-Rankuwa, and that he would therefore probably chalk the Pretoria communication up to the sorcerous assaults of a medicine man. Consequently, it was able to conceal itself temporarily and the Pretoria attack could be viewed as being one of many that had already occurred. It may furthermore be stated that the previously initiated occult attacks provided it with favourable conditions for access. Based on observations, this spirit power has not only attempted to signal its presence but was also able, by means of collaboration, to support the preceding facilitated assaults at *Ga-Rankuwa*.

If we have come to this conclusion, and have attempted to discern the spirits according to their manifestation and have, after the last case, conceded that the spirit power is able to intervene, probably in a calculated way, then the question may be asked: Are spirits able to think? Are they just waiting for a summons, which they then execute according to the request of the person who gave them the mandate? Or might they be operating according to some kind of programme, designed by them, which they subsequently execute in a consciously acting manner? I am of the opinion that they are neither able to think, nor can they act autonomously or even be creative in their own way. They are hardly capable of accomplishing anything on their own. And they are powerless. A spirit power that appears sporadically and can prove to be very powerful does indeed exist, so much so that it can inflict great suffering onto an individual, but this spirit power is unable to think or come up with anything that would be helpful or of benefit to the world or the universe, neither would it be innovatively creative or align itself with the divine order of creation. The spirit power is able to temporarily adapt itself to a given situation, to technological developments as well as the actions of the human mind. It is also able to imitate or copy something already in existence. Everything else that is carried out by spirits and their sorcerous assaults is uncontrollable and destructive in nature. Their aim is to destruct and harm: never constructive, conserving, helping, healing, sophisticated or focussed on a positive objective. Their power exists. It is not personal but rather spirit-like. Like lightning bolts that shoot in dangerous and uncontrollable curves out of a cloud onto the earth, this spirit power can perform its manifestations and assaults in a similar way. It never reveals itself. If it nevertheless does utter a spoken word, something that does not happen in our examples, it is only a mimicry of that which is already known. In spite of all that, it constitutes a reality and possesses a corresponding power. It is able, through this power, to be disruptive and destructive but does, compared to the Creator and his creation, nevertheless only possess a limited ability to demonstrate this power.

Parapsychologists refer to the spirit power's manifestations from the otherworld as "paranormal phenomena". Parapsychology ascribes all spirit manifestations and ghost apparitions to the paranormal sphere, which emanates from human nature. A person releases these spirits from a hitherto unexplored and unknown depth-psychological sphere of his or her soul. Spirits and ghost apparitions are the product of a person's own soul. It is a person's own fault if and when a disaster occurs. A sphere is triggered in the depths of a person's soul, in his or her unconscious – parapsychology speaks of the denominator 'psi' – that releases the apparitions and makes them available to the conscious aspect of the soul. If the emanations that are intimated from a person's unconscious are negative in nature, this can then result in these occultly laden apparitions. Since very little is known of these deep layers of the soul, into which hardly any research could hitherto be done, these obscure apparitions manifest themselves and cause a wide range of problems.

Parapsychologists have however not reached a consensus in their analysis of the deep dimensions of the soul. Thus there are a number of parapsychologists who also locate a spirit power outside of the human unconscious and do therefore not speak exclusively of paranormal phenomena. A spirit power exists. It resides in an otherworld. It takes action as an actual power from a Place Somewhere, which no-one has hitherto been able to explore, examine or even locate.

Writing on Satanism, B. Wenisch states that these apparitions are "occurrences that cannot be explained with the laws of classical science and are therefore, in many instances and to this day, attributed to spirits from the otherworld."[42] The spirits of the otherworld are

---

[42] Op. cit., p. 83. – '... handelt es sich um Vorgänge, die nach den Gesetzmäßigkeit-

located somewhere. Upon their emergence from this Place Some-where they approach humans. They avail themselves primarily of the human psyche. "Together with many parapsychologists, one may venture to put forward the hypothesis that paranormal phenomena can, for the most part, be traced back to the deep psychological powers of the human soul which, even though they are not identical to the psychic dimensions normally referred to as the unconscious, can nonetheless only have an effect by way of the latter."[43] Wenisch, too, leaves the issue of spirits open for contemplation. We agree with his inference, however, that spirits are not to be equated with the unconscious, but that they can approach the human unconscious and use it for their purposes.

The meaning of the assaults of *Ga-Rankuwa* and Pretoria remains the same throughout. The assaulted person must capitulate. He must not resist evil; he must leave *Ga-Rankuwa*. For as long as he resides in that place in *Ga-Rankuwa* that is occupied by the spirit power, evil will stalk him. Boundaries are of no consequence whatsoever. Evil is not limited by state- or neighbourhood boundaries. It is a unitary, evil spirit power that remains unchecked by physical boundaries or na-tional borders.[44]

Aside from the Pretoria assault, which was brought about by physical contact, the suicide of *Rrapula* also needs to be included in this inci-

---

en der klassischen Naturwissenschaften nicht erklärbar sind und die man de-swegen auch heute noch vielfach auf Geister aus dem Jenseits ... zurückführt.'

[43] Op. cit., p. 83-84. – 'Mit vielen Parapsychologen darf man die Hypothese wagen, dass die paranormalen Phänomene zu einem großen Teil auf Tiefenkräfte der menschlichen Seele zurückgehen, die zwar nicht mit den für gewöhnlich als das Unbewußte bezeichneten psychischen Dimensionen identisch sind, sich aber doch nur durch sie auswirken können.'

[44] Examples have been reported – I personally know of two incidents – of Africans who had been given a free study place at a university or were ministering to a Eu-ropean congregation as an exchange pastor, who were pursued by the evil spirits of their home country, incited by the envy of one or several relatives to harass and torment them. These examples, which are merely adduced to second what has been said, are not intended to elicit recriminations. They underscore the point that nothing prevents the spirits that appear in South Africa from pursuing their objec-tives, even in far-away Europe.

dent. There is no doubt at all that a connection exists between these two events. Both assaults were carried out by the same evil force. The severity of the assaults is not the same. At the time of his death *Rrapula* had, through his external circumstances, become vulnerable to taking the decision to end his life. The evil power used this circumstance as an opportunity to tempt him into ending his life. He succumbed to this temptation. This provides the evil force with a show of success, which it then communicates to its second assault victim. This communication frightens the missionary. Its aim is furthermore to convey to him that this evil force is capable of being a powerful accessory to a person's premature death. I asked *Rrapula's* mother when her son went missing and how much later they found him; when comparisons were subsequently drawn as to the possible time of his death, the time shortly after seven o'clock in the evening came into consideration.

The final example deals with an incident that involves a recent, scantily researched phenomenon that is only known and has only been observed in Southern Africa.

5. *Thapelo ya Sephiri* / The mysterious night service

After the spirit troubles had begun in *Ga-Rankuwa* and the number of apparitions were on the increase, I decided to not only withstand them, but also to find out more about the matter. During my subsequent broad-based investigations into the subject of spirit apparitions, my attention was drawn to a matter into which little scientific research has hitherto been done and which, as far as is known, has only occurred in the regions of South Africa and *Botswana*.[45]

---

[45] All studies conducted, of whatever kind, into ghost and spirit apparitions have hitherto been met with scepticism and reservations by humanities scholars. This has to do with the phenomenon of spirits per se. Spirit apparitions are rather difficult to study. If one particular study actually manages to be successful, it merely serves to throw up many new questions, resulting in findings that remain open-ended. Humans have as yet not acquired a level of knowledge which will enable them to comprehend the deeper layers of the soul, as well as space and time beyond their earthly life. It is for this reason that a probe into the spirit world does, for the most part, not progress beyond certain suppositions and assumptions. The field of parapsychology, which specialises in spirit and ghost apparitions, is a hun-

I was now also interested in the *"thapelo ya sephiri"*, the clandestine prayer. Even though I had worked among the *Batswana* for a quite a number of years, had lived, prayed and celebrated with them, and had also resided only in their midst, I had never come across the term *"thapelo ya sephiri"*. I wanted to know what the *"thapelo ya sephiri"* was all about. Could it be that people from the surrounding area had never heard of it either? That is how it seemed at first when I asked all those German colleagues of whom I assumed that they might have a more detailed knowledge of the deeper thoughts and beliefs of the *Batswana*. Things changed immediately, however, when I questioned some African colleagues in this regard. Almost all of them were aware of this matter.

The experiences I gathered on the *"thapelo ya sephiri"* are by no means complete. I eventually abandoned my investigations into this matter. The reasons for this will be provided later. The *"thapelo ya sephiri"* is a special kind of worship service that is celebrated at night. The ceremony starts before midnight. According to Schutte, who is currently probably still the only academic to have launched an investigation into the *"thapelo ya sephiri"* and subsequently wrote an article on it, the people in *Soweto* who have gathered for the Saturday night ceremony start proceedings between 8 pm and 10:30 pm. The worship service goes on for several hours and is concluded in the early hours of Sunday morning.[46]

All participants are emphatically urged to promise not to divulge anything about the ceremony or the goings-on to any other person. In *Soweto*, a guard stands at the entrance of the house where the nocturnal ceremony is taking place; each participant has to provide him with a code word to prove that he or she is a member. No bystanders or interested persons are admitted. The small group of worshippers holds its ceremony neither in a church nor outside under a tree or on the banks of a river, as many of the independent church communities of South Africa do at night or over weekends. These small groups of *"thapelo ya sephiri"*-worshippers, only one meeting of which could be observed by my informants to have taken place in the villages and

---

dred years old already but is still fighting to receive academic recognition by being granted a chair at a university.

[46] Op. cit., p. 252.

identifiable locations of up to 30,000 inhabitants,[47] hold their worship services – containing both Christian and traditional religious elements – in the homes of their members and, almost exclusively, in the home of the leader, who can be male or female. The fact that the meeting does neither take place in a church nor in a public or open space but rather in the home of the group leader facilitates the promise of secrecy. Something concerning Mrs So-and-so happens at her house. Mrs So-and-so has a personal interest in the matter and would not like word of it to be passed on. This has to be respected. This nocturnal ceremony of sorts is moreover not something that everyone would like to participate in.

For most people the nocturnal ceremonies with their secret content hold no particular attraction. They are not particularly interested in seeking to satisfy their religious needs and human desires in a place where night is turned into day and where the Almighty God and the spirits can be worshipped on the same platform, except in some cases where their curiosity got the better of them.

In each of the three cases that I was told about, the leaders were women. In one of the cases a married couple had joined the group. A large part of the leader's responsibilities was almost immediately transferred to the husband. In the patriarchal structure of Batswana society, according to old tradition and in all spheres of life, it is the man who is entrusted with the responsibility of leadership in areas beyond the domestic realm.

One of our parishioners, Mrs X, takes part in the meetings in *Ga-Rankuwa*. She is the daughter of an invested prayer woman of the Lutheran congregation. Mrs X is ill. She has been suffering from headaches for quite some time and no longer attends the church service. During the nocturnal *"thapelo ya sephiri"*-meetings, attempts at healing the sick are also conducted. Mrs X has been told as much. She wants to be healed. That is why she attends those nocturnal meetings, something she is unable to deny. But when she is asked as to what takes place at those meetings, she refuses to answer. She is not allowed to provide any kind of information or furnish anybody

---

[47] In *Soweto* – a city of 2 million inhabitants – there are said to be 35 groups in existence, each consisting of around 25 adults.

with particulars about the meeting and the nocturnal *"thapolo ya sephiri"* worship services. This secret matter constitutes a taboo for Mrs X, too. She wishes to be rid of her severe headaches. Thus she has to adhere to and believe in the rules and prescripts of the *"thapelo ya sephiri"*. If she had no faith in that which was promised to her, her notion of healing would come asunder. Therefore, she counters any query for information about the secret society with the categorical reply: "We are not allowed to talk about the nocturnal meetings" (*ga go buiwe ka ditirelo tsa bosigo*).

Another participant is more forthcoming. One of my old friends, Mr Y, resides in the countryside, is a church elder and will later become school principal and serve on every church committee. His participation at the nocturnal worship services is not determined by his desire for healing, but solely by his interest in taking part and being present when something of a religious nature is offered that is out of the ordinary. But he also wants to know and find out why a small group of Christians has moved its worship service to take place at night. Consequently, his participation at the nocturnal meetings is short-lived. While his wife, who visited these meetings together with him, refuses to provide any kind of information, Mr Y tells me the following: "The invitation to and participation in the *'thapelo ya sephiri'* is based on trust. It was always just a small group of people who participated in the ceremonies. You meet up in the dark and you leave in the dark. Only adults take part. The worship service is held in the house of a member. In our case it was the house of the leader. A room in the house is cleared for this purpose. There must be enough space. Several candles are placed on the floor in the middle of the room. The participants go and dance around the lit candles. There is singing and praying and Bible verses are interpreted. Everyone prays by themselves, out loud or softly. God, Jesus Christ and the ancestors are called upon in the same manner. Each supplicant calls out the names of his or her own ancestors. Healing prayers are recited and healings conducted, but I cannot say anything about that; there were no healings during the time I participated."

The *"thapelo ya sephiri"* is celebrated only at night. Why must Christians congregate during the night when there is no danger of persecution? Ostensible answers like the following could be provided: Christianity and ancestral worship are irreconcilable with one another. The official churches[48] oppose any kind of ancestral worship during church services. In order not to have to exclude the ancestors, however, and to evade being criticised for mixing these two religions, the worship service is moved to the night time. Another reason might be the following: During the night, evil spirits are at work and witches perform their magic. By holding the worship service in the night, the evil spirits and witches are counteracted and given short shrift. Both reasons should not summarily be dismissed out of hand.

In his study, Schutte found that the nocturnal ceremonies in *Soweto* provide the participants with something that helps them to protect their homes and families from the assaults of magic and witchcraft.[49] They take ash from the fire that cooked the sacrificial meat for the ancestors and smear it onto the windows; they also take sea sand, blessed by the leader of the group, and scatter it on the property of the group member. Both procedures serve to prevent the advance of evil spirits and witches. Still, the actual reason for these nocturnal ceremonies may be found somewhere else. I received an indication as to where this reason may be found from a person who was able to observe these goings-on from the outside.

A prayer woman[50] of our church, who was able to observe these nocturnal ceremonies and therefore had information about the participants and members of the *"thapelo ya sephiri"*, told me the following about the same group which was attended by Mr Y in a village in the remote parts of the then Western Transvaal: The participants of that particular *"thapelo ya sephiri"*, who are simultaneously part of a group of local prayer women, are told to render themselves particularly conspicuous at the weekly church gatherings of the prayer women. During the Bible interpretation sessions these women are emphatic about their own interpretation, pushing themselves to the fore, thereby plac-

---

[48] Most notably the Protestant churches, while the Catholic church may possibly have a different opinion on the matter. Experiences with a Catholic priest in this regard could confirm this assumption.

[49] Op. cit., p. 254.

[50] A prayer woman is a member of the congregation who joins a women's group with specially defined responsibilities, a group that dedicates itself mainly to prayer. A member of such a women's group is identified by her distinct clothing. Prayer women can be found in all major church denominations in South Africa.

ing more value on their interpretation than on that of others. This observation points to the fact that the actions of the members of the *"thapelo ya sephiri"* appear to be those of devout and privileged African Christians. These actions may have a specific significance.

Schutte goes into more detail about the hierarchical structure and makeup of the *"thapelo ya sephiri"*-movement. The different levels, the regulations and special positions that have been put into place come in useful for many Africans; but not for the Africans only. One is inclined to associate the structural makeup of the *"thapelo ya sephiri"*-movement with that of the Jehovah's Witnesses, and, due to their special status, with the Jewish Qumran sect, or else with every person who considers him- or herself to be someone more special than his or her fellow human being.

According to Schutte, the system of the movement is structured in such a way that a member starts at the bottom and aspires to reach the top. The rise to the top is a gradual one and, after death, continues almost infinitely in the spirit realm.

New aspirants are not granted membership immediately. They first have to demonstrate the sincerity of their application. During their probation period the aspirants are obliged to present themselves to the group with testimonials, their prayer and their faith. After having survived their probation period, aspirants may be admitted to the group. Admission takes place with a nocturnal sacrificial ceremony or, in case of illness, with a nocturnal healing ceremony, which can also not be performed without paying the ancestors their sacrificial dues. A sacrificial sheep is slaughtered. The fact that the sacrificial animal has to be a sheep is possibly of special significance to the movement. Aspirants who want to join the movement are referred to as *"dipodi"* (goats), while full members are referred to as *"dinku"* (sheep). To sacrifice a sheep could therefore have the symbolic meaning that, after new members have been admitted into the movement, they are elevated to the proper and better status, and can possibly also be associated with Christ, the shepherd of his sheep. Once new members have been admitted, they enjoy all the rights of the group. The new member can become a prayer leader, a pastor or even the spiritual leader of the group. The matters pertaining to the group are delegated from the top downwards.

A similar pyramid can be discerned in the spirit world. God is the supreme being. The group below him consists of Jesus Christ, the angels and the apostles, among whom Christ is seen as being the oldest brother. The bottom-most group comprises all the ancestors. Cross-connections exist between both worlds on the respective levels. Thus the spiritual leader will receive his or her revelations directly from Jesus Christ, for instance, while the ordinary members are commandeered by the ancestral spirits. All members will eventually become ancestors. It is inappropriate to mourn a person's death. Mourning obstructs the path of the deceased on their way to the spirit world.

Due to their ranking within the group, all members are deemed to be someone special. They belong to an elite group of Christians. By rising up to the respective next level, each member is placed into a communal hierarchy with others, which leads to a sense of solidarity on the one hand, and urges members to see themselves as above those who are still ranked below them on the other. At least, that is how one might interpret the fact that the above-mentioned prayer woman, after having risen in the ranks of the *"thapelo ya sephiri"*-movement, now showcases and asserts her superior position and advancement in front of her fellow Christians during daily church activities.

Let us cast our minds back to *Ga-Rankuwa*. It needs to be mentioned at this point that the missionary from *Ga-Rankuwa* has been transferred to the little town of Brits, 30 km away. And the spirits of *Ga-Rankuwa* have followed him there, to be sure, initially showing their presence by a low-level apparition. However, after the missionary extended a tacit yet clear peace offering to his adversary, who had probably orchestrated the sorcerous assaults, the spirits did not come back. I will refer to this development again at a later stage.

When it appeared as though the spirits of *Ga-Rankuwa* had left for good, others soon began creeping in. The assumption can once again be made that magic played a major role. After I had set myself the task of investigating the *"thapelo ya sephiri"* more thoroughly, I paid Mrs X another visit. This time, too, just as on previous visits, she refused to provide me with any information. Her health still showed no signs of improvement.

During that time, I received word that Mrs Z was the leader of the *"thapelo ya sephiri"* in *Bapong*, not far from Brits. Mrs Z was a prayer woman in the Methodist church. In the hope that I would be able to glean information from her or even be allowed to attend a *"thapelo ya sephiri"* in *Bapong*, I made several attempts at contacting Mrs Z. I never had a conversation with her. Time and again, Mrs Z refused to see me.

While I continued to occupy myself with the *"thapelo ya sephiri"*, the first mysterious assaults came ever closer to our house in Brits. They came from the outside. A renewed despatch had been launched. Again it was a bird that had been despatched into the dark night, to disturb and possibly even cause material damage. It was my wife who heard it first, during two consecutive nights, as it perched in a tree close to our house, uttering its magical, composite sounds. The following night it flew into the large window pane of our bedroom. It caused a loud, hard bang in the stillness of the night. The window pane did not break, however. The bird flew away. It felt like it was a very specific attack. The bird had chosen the window of the parents' bedroom, even though that side of the house had three additional windows. We realised immediately that it was attacking us with a very specific aim. During the following two nights it perched in a tree again. Its screeching was more subdued, and after a while the despatches ceased altogether.

This was the first time that my wife had been involved in a despatch. She was the first to hear the strange bird. I had not noticed it during the first couple of nights. While my wife had not seen or heard anything of the spirits in *Ga-Rankuwa*, she is the one who witnesses a magical despatch in Brits.

A difference between the assaults of *Ga-Rankuwa* and those in Brits may be discerned: In *Ga-Rankuwa*, the despatch was particularly aimed at the soul of the missionary. A despatch that is aimed at the soul of a person cannot be seen by any other person. This kind of despatch is admittedly initiated by the medicine man, but it is the spirit power itself that executes it. The first despatch in Brits was executed solely by the medicine man. He used his magic expertise to direct the bird towards a specific target, as had been the case in the first example cited above.

After the bewitched night bird had completed its despatch, there was no further disturbance in Brits for a week. After that, however, the sorcerous activity was deployed in a hitherto unfamiliar form. It was focused very specifically on me, and in a most vicious, wicked way. Every time I went to bed at night, the events of the day that I let pass before my mind's eye simply stood still. It was as if those images were riveted in my mind. Up to that point I had not visualised those images that clearly because they had been brought up from the unconscious realms of my soul, images that had been present at all other times too, to be sure, but had been absorbed more unconsciously into my mind. These pictures were frozen. There was no sequence of events. Ordinary images, of the kind that a normal eye records every day, were standing still. They were held captive.[51] A completely bizarre, confounded situation arises when one's visual images are forcibly frozen by sorcerous means. This condition is not in keeping with human nature and existence. Human beings are alive. They are part of creation, having received life from their Creator. Life is a course of events, it moves forward. Sorcery is able to intervene in this process. An intervention of this kind lies within its power but it has no right to intervene in a person's life, forcing it to a standstill. Sorcerous intervention by means of a blockade is neither wanted nor needed.

When I said a prayer in that condition, I felt far away from God. My prayers lacked the strength to overcome that sorcery. I had the impression that I was talking to an impenetrable wall. I also began experiencing a feeling of emptiness. I felt as if sorcery had cast a total spell on my emotions, too. My connection with God had been severed. On those occasions when sorcery had cast such a spell on me the thought of falling asleep also totally dissipated.

When this spell continued over an extended period of time I contemplated what I could do to rid myself of it. Nothing came to mind. One day I told myself: "You have more than enough other work to do. You are not making any progress at the moment with the *'thapelo ya sephiri'* anyhow. Give it up." I thought it over once more and then I gave up my research into this movement. That was the end of the magic spell. In the evenings, the one or other image passed before my inner eyes. The number of images was now much smaller than what

---

[51] Imagine a movie that freezes during any given suspense-filled scene. You want the scene to move on, but nothing happens. The image is frozen just like a photograph. Then imagine that exactly this scenario can happen to you personally.

they had been during that time of sorcerous intervention. Most of them had once again been relegated to my unconscious mind, where they remained hidden. And the minor visions and every-day events appeared and moved on. I felt relieved and released at the same time. My life in the evenings took on its natural course again.

One may deliberate anew as to whether I had talked myself into these sorcerous disruptions in the evening. Perhaps my thoughts, due to whatever circumstances that weighed heavily on me, penetrated my psychological processes by way of suggestion? The images that passed through my mind were forced to a standstill by my own will due to some unresolved culpability on my part. One can explore these issues in many different ways. In doing so, one should however not neglect to take the antecedents to this intervention into consideration. This final sorcerous despatch commenced by the targeted assault of a night bird, first noticed by my wife, a person who had stood on the side-lines during all the other incidents. After the despatched night bird had done its groundwork, I was attacked directly.

This final example must also be placed into a certain context. In order to provide an explanation for all examples, beginning with the first one, then *Ga-Rankuwa* and finally Brits, one must take the interconnectedness and above all the context into account. The context in this instance is a collective society informed by magical thinking; a society that is admittedly geared towards change, but still condones a vast array of phenomena dating back to ancient times. If the individual incidents are placed into a larger context, a psychological explanation will no longer suffice if the measures that were usually taken and brought in from the outside to instigate the various incidents are taken into account.

In Part Three, following below, the spirits and evil powers are brought into relation with the Christian faith. In doing so, my appraisal of the issue will receive initial priority. The behaviour of the *Batswana* Christians concerning this fundamental evil of theirs will be discussed. I will reflect on matters of faith. In conclusion I will pose the question as to whether the manifestations of the myriad of spirits from the otherworld are indeed proof of an afterlife.

III. Overcoming Evil

1. Afflictions of faith

a) The example:

Spirits not only take a toll on one's soul. Sorcery can also be deployed by them on a vulnerable part of the body of an assaulted person.

I cast my mind far back into the past. Since my youth, probably towards the end of my school career, I experienced a feeling of unease every time the thought of death by hanging or strangulation entered my mind. This fear, which I had long since forgotten, was utilised by the spirits as a new point of entry at *Ga-Rankuwa*. One day, when I already had started fighting the evil spirits, I experienced emotions that were entirely foreign to me. The onset of these unpleasant feelings occurred in my chest area. They moved upwards. The further up they moved, the more intense they became. They reached their climax in my neck area. Their intensity was particularly forceful and strong, so much so that they induced slight disfigurations in the lower half of my face. These strangulation assaults, contracting my neck, occurred during the daytime or in the evening, never during the night when I was asleep. They arose and then subsided again. On many occasions these assaults occurred when I was occupying myself with books that told stories of spirits and apparitions of ghosts or else attempted to analyse and investigate them.

b) The explanation

Do psychological aspects come into play during these strangulation attacks? Was it merely a weakness on my behalf, that I was not able to deal with an old problem? Psychology might be considered to provide an answer in this instance. To dismiss this incident as being solely psychogenic in origin would however be too superficial. I had lived with this psychological weakness for years and never had a problem with it here in Africa. Therefore, the new environment I found myself in must be taken into consideration. My environment was charged with sorcery and spirits. Consequently, it may be assumed that the spirits picked my psychological weakness as a convenient point of entry to bring up something from the hidden aspects of my soul, in order to weaken their opponent even further.

The incident described above has caused me great embarrassment. While having my own thoughts about the spirit apparitions, thinking that they would stop one day, or that a way would be found to expose the powers and persons that had formed a mutual pact, I searched for a speedy way to rid myself of these inconvenient strangulation attacks. While contemplating this it became clear to me that I could no longer rely only on myself, my physical strength and my prayers. I needed help from outside. I thought of the help that my friends might provide. But those friends that first came to mind were out of the question; the stories of the spirit apparitions at *Ga-Rankuwa* had done the rounds already. Most of my friends thought that those events were funny and joked about them. So, for understandable reasons, I was unable to put these friends on my shortlist. I chose a missionary who was known to me as having a great amount of prayer experience, and who had had dealings with a poltergeist and other spirits in his own house as well. This missionary lived quite far away from me at the time.

I was well aware of the fact that there is praying, and then there is Praying. There are all kinds of gifts in the Kingdom of God. There are many kinds of prayers, and amongst those who pray there are those who are more blessed than others. That missionary had been particularly blessed by God; he was an exceptionally gifted prayer. After he had prayed for me the strangulation attacks that subsequently arose became less powerful. They became tolerable. My face no longer showed any outward signs of contortion during an attack. The thought crossed my mind to have these strangulating powers eliminated altogether. After a few months I paid another visit to my intercessor. To my surprise I found that my friend was no longer interested in complying with my repeated request to pray for my affliction yet again. "I should content myself with my situation, other people also had their burdens to carry", he said, but did nonetheless pray for me. However, these prayers remained unanswered. Disappointed, I travelled the long journey home again.

Of course I continued to reflect on what measures I could take to rid myself of the remainder of the strangulation attacks. I considered my options at length. Then, one day, it occurred to me that the anxieties I experienced before a strangulation attack probably went way back, and that they had started when I was working at a place where the father of one of my classmates had hanged himself in a tree next door. The fear of being strangled could possibly have insinuated itself into my psyche on that occasion. On my next home leave in Germany I visited the place from where I thought that my anxieties originated. After I had reached the place I began talking. I spoke quietly to myself, seeing that I was not alone. There were other people as well. Did they notice anything? I said the following: "I do not wish to hang onto the fear that I internalised in this place a long time ago. I never wanted it anyway. I do not want it now. I no longer want it at all. It does not belong to me. It does not belong to who I am. I have been created better. It must stay here. I belong to another, to my Lord, who is good." I don't know why I said those things. I realise in hindsight that I should have immediately started the first sentences of this psychological conversation with a prayer. Well, since then the strangulation attacks that started somewhere in my chest, gradually increasing in intensity while approaching the neck area, have totally disappeared. During the ensuing weeks and months, I could hardly believe that it was all over, but it was. To this day nothing of the sort has cropped up again.

My physical life returned to normal. My personal life of faith, too, had been put right again after it had been challenged by spirits in many different ways, especially during their initial appearances.

2. A little conversion

a) The example:

Once evil has been tapped into by those experimenting with sorcery, this can have many different consequences for those people for whom it is intended. There is no doubt in my mind that the person who orchestrated the assaults of the manifestations in *Ga-Rankuwa* and who started everything is a member of the congregation. It was the intention of this person to teach the missionary a clear lesson in the traditional African way. After eight months and during a heated discussion – we were alone in my office – this person raised a warning finger, saying the words *"o tla se bona"* = you just wait and see.

At the time I didn't know that *"o tla se bona"* is a common saying, used by someone to terminate a discussion in order to seek revenge by means of magic and sorcery.

When I offered resistance over a protracted period of time, this person thought of something else. My reputation was sullied in an underhanded way towards my superiors. This defamation continued for quite some time. My superiors accepted the complaints without ever consulting me on the matter. A transfer was proposed. Neither the congregation nor the missionary concerned were consulted. As far as the superiors are concerned, this procedure is justified in the context of an authoritarian-oriented African church. At that point in time, when a certain person already had a notion that the missionary was to be transferred, the spirit despatches were reduced. And their assaults were less intense.

A few days before my transfer, another member of the congregation whom I had told about the spirit apparitions said to me: "The spirits will follow you. They are not bound to one location. They will look for you and find you." And so it was: it did not take long before they had traced us to Brits, a town 30 km away. They began harmlessly enough, just as they had three years ago in *Ga-Rankuwa*. The knocking on the bedroom door was much softer. It was as soft as it had been in *Ga-Rankuwa* right towards the end. I actually wanted to forget everything, to draw a line under everything.

While contemplating these matters, two things struck me. For one thing, I was not interested in carrying the huge burden placed on me by the spirits yet again. For another, I realised how foolishly I had conducted myself during that entire time. I had tried from the start, after the spirits had begun assaulting me, to ward them off and defeat them by my own strength. And I had been more or less successful in doing that, to be sure. But I had also experienced their strange power. They had rudely awakened me, had unsettled me in many respects and had caused a myriad of other problems.

A considerable amount of rage had settled in my heart. I hated the man who I thought had orchestrated everything. I realised that I hated someone, that I was incredibly angry with him, that I had an enemy whom I someday wished to pay back in kind. But then I also realised that I had moved far away from God's commandments. The word "love" entered my mind, something I had discerned so little of during the past few years. I also realised that Jesus didn't say: "Hate your enemy and look for an opportunity to defeat him." Jesus had said the exact opposite: "Love your enemies, do good to those who hate you." I had diverged from Jesus' teachings so much, but at the same time I wanted to be his disciple. I had sinned and offended my Lord, Jesus. I should repent and change my behaviour and attitude. I needed to make a new start. As this change of heart went through my mind I began thinking positively, living with good thoughts. When I then also began speaking highly of that particular person, of whom I am convinced to this day that he had a hand in the spirit incursions, and began praising his positive side in front of others, the spirit appearances decreased in frequency until, finally, they totally disappeared.

b) The explanation

The question may be asked once again: Were the manifestations in *Ga-Rankuwa* just of a psychological nature after all? The missionary had constructed them himself in the depths of his heart. His unconscious mind absorbed the unresolved problems that arose, playing them back during the night. All spirit manifestations that presented themselves originated from within himself. If he had rather countered those tensions in a more relaxed way, if he had responded to his adversary with love right from the start, the spirits would not have appeared. Maybe, one could argue, maybe everything would have turned out differently. There is no guarantee that things would have been different or that conflicts wouldn't have arisen at all. In my capacity as leader of the congregation I was also unable to meet the numerous excessive demands made on me by that particular person in his relentless manner. But now everything happened as has been described on the preceding pages. What can one say about that?

My own explanation as to what occurred is the following: Some of the manifestations in *Ga-Rankuwa* were admittedly of a psychological nature, but this subdomain that is derived from psychological forces does not imply a desire of the psyche, i.e. it did not emanate from the psyche but was rather brought to its attention. The stress that my predecessors in *Ga-Rankuwa* had previously suffered from the same spirits was of a far more serious nature. In each instance, the soul of a person admitted and accommodated them. One may add that the soul of a missionary can be just as susceptible to such instigated spirit disturbances as are the large number of Africans who have been affected by them. My unconscious mind, too, had an opening which was utilised by the spirits to gain access. They executed their incursion during the night in their particular way, just as they had already done with four other predecessors in the same parsonage; of these incidents, just one was not aimed at the pastor but rather at his wife.

After my consciousness had registered this incursion and I realised the deception that the spirits had performed on me, I refused to be taken in by the delusion and – how could it be otherwise – opted for resistance.

The battle for the unconscious mind is being fought on two fronts. The spirits intervene. They affect and burden the unconscious with the ultimate aim of seizing it in its entirety. The missionary offers resistance. He attempts in his own way to prevent them from coming back again and again through prayer and deliberations. In the end it is apparently by chance that the battle is won; the transfer from *Ga-Rankuwa* to Brits heralds in a change.

One may reflect on the possibility that the battle with the spirits would have continued if a transfer had not taken place. Or would something have changed, and how would this have affected the outcome? Apart from a transfer I could not hope for any other solution to my difficulties from my church superiors. Their answer in overcoming problems of this nature was inadequate. The church had proved this in other similar cases known to me, as well as with my predecessor who had lived in the same house. My predecessor told me that he had to endure great suffering because of those spirit assaults.

To conclude the conflicts of *Ga-Rankuwa* we may turn to the apostle Paul. Paul has a great interest in the precepts of God concerning the "inner being". He has been liberated by Jesus from the Law and the "oldness of the letter". He nevertheless has a yoke to bear. Paul struggles with the Law. In Romans 7:7 he says: "What then shall we say? That the law is sin? By no means! Yet if it had not been for the law, I would not have known sin. For I would not have known what it is to covet if the law had not said, 'You shall not covet.'" Paul has learnt what it means to covet through the precepts of the Lord. It seems as though he is quite confused in what he wants to say, for he goes on (v.15): "For I do not understand my own actions. For I do not do what I want, but I do the very thing I hate." He wanted to do something totally different to that which he actually does if covetousness/desire had not seduced him, namely the complete opposite. In verse 19 he says: "For I do not do the good I want, but the evil I do not want is what I keep on doing." Is what Paul is saying hard to understand? It is indeed hard to understand. But then again it is not entirely incomprehensible. Probably every adult, experienced Christian is able to relate to what Paul is saying in Romans 7. Everybody has had first-hand experience of what Paul is saying. How many good as well as bad things happen, emanating from the unconscious mind and informed by desire, of which one only becomes aware and cognisant much later? During one of his lectures, the philosopher Weizsäcker once said in a lecture at Hamburg University that most human actions emanate from the unconscious mind and that, by comparison, only a few are controlled by the conscious mind. Paul attributes this to desire, saying that it affects the Law, thereby giving rise to sin. It unsettles Paul that his desire leads him into sin. He takes issue on this matter with the Lord. He goes before God with his desire and professes that he is a sinful man.

Does it not also fall under covetousness to want to acquire power and gain advantage over others by seeking out and utilising magical powers? A 19th century writer had the following to say on the topic of coveting magical power: "Sorcery is appealing to most people as they view it as being a preternatural means of satisfying their passions."[52] Paul says that the Law has power, but that it is desire that leads him into temptation. In a great number of cases the spirit power is contacted from the outside. By desiring/coveting it, humans draw the spirit power towards them, either by addressing or tapping into it, or by summoning it with a spell. After its presence has thus been requested, it makes its appearance. After it has been roped in

---

[52] Levi, p. 37 – 'Für die meisten ist Magie anziehend, weil sie in ihr ein außergewöhnliches Mittel zur Befriedigung ihrer Leidenschaft sehen.'

to concoct a plan, sinful actions will emerge via the spirit power, just as they do via the Law, according to Paul. One difference is that, whereas someone who takes issue with the Law is confronted by the living God, this cannot be said of a person who has decided to employ sorcery as a means to deal with his or her daily life. If sorcery is not coveted it remains harmless. If someone wishes for magical powers to come to them, they are invoking these powers. This can have devastating consequences for someone else.

When the spirit power has released a manifestation from its arsenal, it unsettles the person at whom it is directed. That person then finds him- or herself embroiled in a battle they did not wish for. They get drawn into a power struggle with sin during which they, due to their limited power, will be in an inferior position. An alien power has made advances toward them that is not in accordance with their nature, their capabilities or their knowledge. Their strength alone will therefore not suffice to be able to withstand this power. Let us hear what Paul has to say once more. The apostle is no stranger to these alien powers either. He does not fear them; but he does warn against them in Ephesians 6:12: "For we do not wrestle against flesh and blood, but against the rulers, against the authorities, … against the spiritual forces of evil in the heavenly places."

3. Of Christians among the *Batswana*

In hindsight I am glad that all that sorcery is now behind me. I have, with the things that happened to me in the supernatural world of spirits, acquired experiences that only a few missionaries have experienced for themselves. I can understand how my fellow Christians among the *Batswana* are suffering under this burden of sorcery and witchcraft they are forced to endure. I feel sorry for them. Some of them have no idea as to how to rid themselves of this burden. They accept it as their fate and let it happen. The ancestors, their deceased forebears whom they believe to be alive and wielding power, have condoned everything that happens. The ancestors know what is beneficial. The ancestors will interfere and help if they choose to do so. If they choose not to help, then there is simply no other alternative. Then the person who has been afflicted by sorcery must simply waste away and expect to die a premature death.

When sorcery is suspected it is traditional custom to plan a counter-strike. This is undertaken, not by the victims of sorcery themselves, but rather vicariously by their family members. It is not only the individual who suffers but the collective as a whole. Advice is given to the extended family as to what means it will employ to execute an equally clandestine counterattack. The predicament they then face is quite profound. Both sides have employed the services of a medicine man, who initiates the retaliatory attacks on the other family. These reciprocal attacks are sometimes drawn out over weeks and months, or even an entire year. Even if legal proceedings should have been initiated with the local council, the attacks often only cease after blood has been shed on one of the two sides, or someone has been killed on either side.[53]

The Christians among the *Batswana* are not excluded from these sorcerous assaults. I met quite a number of Christians who refrained from initiating this kind of retaliation. Only a few of them succeed, through prayer and faith, to overcome these manifestations of sorcery. Experience has taught them that a sorcerous despatch possesses the power to make a person physically ill, and that this illness, sorcerous in origin, will frequently present itself in a specific part of the body during its initial stages, in a leg or the stomach area, for instance. At the onset of such an illness, the afflicted person will first be taken to a medical doctor of Western origin. They might also be taken to a herbalist[54] for treatment, who administers biological remedies to them. They hope that the medical doctor and the healer will be able to tell them that the illness is attributable to physical or psychological causes, and that the patient will be on the mend soon. If neither of them succeeds in healing the patient with their expertise and their medicines, then all doubt has been removed that they are dealing with an illness that has been sent by a sorcerer. When they realise that the ailing person cannot be cured by a herbalist or by Western medicine, the *Batswana* Christians approach this problem in different ways. Some of them only consult a traditional medicine man after the illness has already progressed significantly, who will then proceed to analyse the bewitchment by means of small medi-

---

[53] Cf. G. and E. Richter, pp. 66-68.

[54] A healer who has specialised in herbalism.

umistic objects like bones of wild animals or sea shells and recommend a course of action to the patient. Then there are other Christians who, on the basis of their faith and for many different reasons, will not seek the help of their local medicine man. Even though someone who consults a medicine man has a better chance of ridding him- or herself of a sorcerous affliction – seeing that the latter is able to make use of a counterspell – the end result is usually a grave illness on both sides. With both these approaches it needs to be emphasised that, as a rule, Christians will not initiate any reciprocal measures in the old traditional way, as was also still the case in the time of Jesus when Jews were faced with an enemy. Generally speaking, the Christians among the *Batswana* don't adhere to the rule of "an eye for an eye" or "a tooth for a tooth", the *lex talionis* (law of *talion* = retaliation authorised by law) of the Israelites.[55] Their primary interest is in finding a cure for their ailment. It should also be emphasised that a number of Christians never recover again, and die prematurely of the sorcerously initiated illness.

There are enough examples that attest to the fact that someone who was made ill by sorcerous and magical means never recovered again. I have seen examples of this in the congregations I ministered to, and from pastoral counselling sessions in hospitals. When a patient, lying in hospital, tells his pastor: "The doctors can't help me. They don't know what kind of illness I have. I would really just like to go home", then usually the patient, as well as the doctor and the hospital counsellor, knows that the illness is not of physical but rather of sorcerous origin.

I have the greatest respect for the Christians among the *Batswana*, who are afflicted by sorcery in various ways because they conduct themselves differently from the people amongst whom they live and who are more entrenched in their traditional ways. Sorcery continues to form a part of collective popular belief. It is deployed when an individual becomes overwhelmed by personal insult, envy or hunger for power and seeks to take revenge by means of a clandestine attack.

---

[55] Haag, p. 109f.

It would make little sense to try and abolish the practise of sorcery in a short period of time as long as a better substitute cannot be created within the construct of popular belief. And besides, who would be in a position and have the authority to re-engineer, as it were, an ancient and entrenched arcane tradition within a short period of time? Popular belief intuitively continues to comprise, approve of and lay claim to sorcerous practises. It would however make sense to put a stop to a witch doctor's activities and to scrutinise and monitor the medicine men, so that they perform their activities in public rather than in secret. There are only a few places where attempts have been made in this regard, for instance in the *Batswana* settlement of Jericho, which is a step in the right direction, but which has nonetheless not yielded any significant results.

4. A different kind of faith

Among the *Batswana*, the practise of sorcery continues to constitute an active means of attracting, along long-held traditional and secret pathways, a power that is deployed to teach one person a lesson and to provide gratification for another. According to ancient religious concepts, sorcery forms part of the set of beliefs that can only be deployed via the traditional medicine man (*ngaka* = priest, doctor, healer), who acts as intermediary between the two worlds of the ancestors and the living. The medicine man is fully aware of his actions in his capacity as mediator between the living and the ancestors. He always acts in the interest of the ancestors. Hence he cannot commit an evil act, according to his conception of himself, even if he is able to inflict serious harm on others. Since he considers himself as being an intermediary, he takes no responsibility for an evil act. It is always the ancestors who allow everything. The responsibility lies with them and not with the medicine man, who believes in them and whom he trusts implicitly. The medicine man is an instrument of the ancestors. Everything is possible as long as he continues to view himself as an instrument of the ancestors. Only a small number of medicine men and women are prepared to ponder on the possibility of rejecting a mandate given to them which may lead to dire consequences. I once asked a medicine woman, who regularly attended the church services and who spoke openly to me about her patients' concerns, how many people came to her with interpersonal disappointments or transgressions, requesting of her to cast an evil spell on someone: "There are many. I always manage to turn these people away; but they always go away disappointed."

Sorcery still forms a part of collective thought. The world view of the *Batswana* is informed by the collective. In the collective, one person lives for the other. One person will act vicariously on behalf of another. Nobody is left to fend for themselves. Every individual is bound to the community. On a horizontal, socio-cultural level the community is everything. Everyone falls in line with their individual abilities. The individual adheres to the precepts of the community. The community lives through him or her. The individual makes or breaks the community. It sets the boundaries and fills in the gaps. The individual participates in all events. Being a part of the collective, it is the obligation of an individual to attend all feasts that require a sacrifice for or a plea to the ancestors. If no-one gets out of line the community remains intact. If someone should make themselves conspicuous, however, or step out of line, danger lurks. And this danger weakens the community. It suffers a loss of power and standing. Its unity is destroyed. But this unity needs to be restored. Many different avenues are explored in order to restore the unity of the community. One possible avenue is the following: Should the social hierarchy have been infringed on or interpersonal relationships have been broken, it will more often than not be a member of the extended family who will attempt to correct the loss of harmony in the community by consulting a sorcerer. If community life has been disrupted and nothing is undertaken to restore the equilibrium, the living dead (ancestors) in the otherworld will not remain silent. These are, for the most part, benign spirits that should not be woken or disturbed in any way. That is why the community can put its own house in order through the implementation of punitive measures by means of sorcery. In doing so the unity within the community will not only have been restored, but the religious communion that exists with the ancestors will also not have been violated.

At first one might magnanimously consider this way of life, by virtue of its traditional belief system, to provide some kind of help in the social coexistence of a collective, closed society. Be that as it may, this was the path that was taken from time immemorial whenever a breach had occurred within the community. And, to this day, this path is still frequently embarked on when communal life has been disrupted. It can however not be disputed that many families no longer make use of this path. This circumstance has been brought about by various factors, and also by temporal and spiritual changes. Due to the fact that this closed community life has now also broken asunder, the deployment of sorcerous attacks has declined between members of their own extended family, even though cases of this nature do still appear from time to time. These attacks are now being carried out in the neighbourhood, where family members no longer live close to one another as had been the case during earlier times, and as can still be observed in settlements where the dwellings have been constructed in the old traditional style. Other cases of sorcery are known to have spread outside the confines of family ties into certain circles of friends. The belief in sorcery has thereby been extended to communal life in general. Anyone who coexists with their fellow humans for a protracted period of time can become a victim of sorcery; they may offend others who have not overcome their traditional belief in sorcery, and who condone the clandestine path of sorcery to humiliate their fellow human beings or cause them great misery.

Sorcery is evil. A malevolent thought gives rise to it. Not every malevolent thought leads to sorcery. Everybody is capable of doing evil, but not everyone is concerned with sorcery. In Africa, the concept of sorcery is linked to a belief system that was assimilated into collective thought by the forefathers, and which is still utilised along the same age-old path of knowledge. Nobody is forced to initiate or perform sorcerous acts. It is an individual choice whether he or she, leaning towards the old superstitious tendencies, deploys sorcerous means for his or her expediency to achieve an unfavourable outcome for others. The decision always lies with the individual. In the collective it may be an individual or a group who, of their own volition and due to a preceding provocation or simply out of personal interest, have become convinced that they should deploy evil forces to instigate an action.

In its origin, sorcery forms part of the religion of humankind. Sorcery, for its part, presupposes the existence of magic. A differentiation is nowadays made between magic and religion. In Germany, for instance, reference is only rarely made to magic in connection with religion. Magic is dismissed with the comment that it forms part of the sorcerous acts of primitive indigenous peoples. Religious scholars and anthropologists have divergent opinions on the subject of "magic and religion". The subject of "magic and religion" is still not fully clarified. The question remains open as to whether magic and religion once formed a single entity, or whether they should be viewed as having been separate from the start, and, in case of the latter, which one of the two would have taken precedence. K. Beth, who posits the demanding nature of magic, states: "Magic and religion are the antithesis of one another and cannot be reconciled. That is why magic kills religion wherever it has dominion, and why a vibrant religion fights against magic."[56] Or A. Jensen: "Magic and religion are probably equally old, where one has fundamentally nothing to do with the other."[57] I. Paulson, on the other hand, who interprets the concept of magic on a broader basis, declares: "I assert that there exists no clear distinction [between the two]."[58] And: "Thus the concepts of magic and religion are immutably interwoven. In most instances, 'magic and religion' represent the two sides of one and the same rite."[59]

On the basis of my own experiences, my personal sympathies tend to lie more with K. Beth, who addresses the more radical side of magic. Whoever questions the concept of magic in principle, as K. Beth and other authors have done, must put up with the criticism that their judgement lacks objectivity; they view magic through a mirror that is informed by Judaeo-Christian religion. M. and R. Wax are among those authors who award the concept of magic its own world view, a world view that is not sufficiently recognised by the humanities in

---

[56] Op. cit., p. 46. – 'Magie und Religion sind Gegensätze, die sich nicht vereinbaren lassen. Deshalb ertötet die Magie, wo sie herrscht, die Religion, und deshalb kämpft lebendige Religion gegen die Magie.'

[57] Op. cit., p. 294. – 'Magie und Religion sind wahrscheinlich gleich alt und haben im Wesentlichen nichts miteinander zu tun.'

[58] M. and R. Wax, op. cit., p. 372. – 'Ich bestätige, daß es eine klare Trennung … nicht gibt.'

[59] Ibid., p. 374. – 'So ist der Begriff der Magie unwandelbar mit dem der Religion verwoben. In den meisten Fällen stellen 'Magie und Religion' die beiden Seiten ein und desselben Ritus dar.'

the Western world: "It is not merely a matter of the rationalistic world view of the West differing from the world view of magic – it is hostile towards it, as has been proven by the long history of moral and religious crusades and missions of the West against other nations. Judaeo-Christian prophets have decried rituals of magic as being immoral and blasphemous; Western philosophers have disregarded the structure of magical experience as superstition, as 'monstrous hodgepodge'. Consequently, the intrinsic structure of the magical world remains hidden from Western observers, as they have only seen it through their own cultural lenses."[60]

If one can assume that the scope of the concept of magic is broad-based in the world view of African nations, it stands to reason that, in its essence, magic informs the belief system of a people and of individuals as much as religion does. If holding a certain belief is essential to all humans, may we reflect on this belief a little? What does our belief mean to us? Having a belief system is a fundamental aspect of humanity. It is so highly valued that no person can do without it. Belief/faith helps us to conduct our lives, has the ability to alleviate our worries and problems or even disperse them altogether. There is also something attractive about belief/faith, something that inherently transcends human life. Faith restores one's health and refreshes that which is natural. A positive faith enriches the soul with personal relationships and spiritual gifts. Faith also has an ultimate goal. A positive faith attains that goal. Faith triumphs. A positive faith never loses. To believe means to live, really live, and to be a good person, or to aspire to become a good person according to the belief of one's calling, a person who radiates something to the people around him, something that others might still be lacking. A positive faith has an effect on other people. It radiates something that can be accepted by oth-

---

[60] Ibid., p. 351. – 'Die rationalistische Weltsicht des Westens ist von der magischen Weltsicht nicht nur verschieden – sie ist ihr feindlich, wie die lange Geschichte religiöser und moralischer Kreuzzüge und Missionen des Westens gegen andere Völker bewiesen haben. Jüdisch-christliche Propheten haben die magischen Riten als unmoralisch und gotteslästerlich angesehen; westliche Philosophen haben die magische Struktur der Erfahrung als Aberglauben, als 'monströsen Mischmasch' betrachtet. Dementsprechend blieb die innere Struktur der magischen Welt dem westlichen Beobachter verborgen, weil er sie nur durch seine eigene Kulturbrille gesehen hatte.'

ers and is beneficial to the community. Faith does not isolate. Not only is it oriented towards others, but also towards an entity in the hereafter. Belief is spiritual. That is why my belief seeks to connect to spiritual entities. It yearns for spiritual beings and deities. Belief is a beautiful thing that brings joy and adds perspective to one's life. One derives a great deal of pleasure from believing. Belief is a fundamental human concern. It lies at the core of humanity, providing the believer with fresh impetus. One's faith can become the bedrock upon which all disagreements, struggles and frustrations are poured in order to realign them. There also resides in faith an incentive for beauty, love and perfection. Faith imparts a suffused solitude, seeks to find a balanced compromise between two extremes and provides the believer with inner peace. Everything is contained within faith. Faith cannot be compared with anything else, not even love. Love is a product of faith. It is worth one's while to accept and build on the Christian faith.

Let us return to the subject of magic and religion and sum up these two entities of great magnitude with a quote by O. Pettersson: "Magic accepts the existence of supernatural forces much in the same way as religion does. Both have their roots in the supernal world. Both 'magic' and 'religion' originate from the same basis, namely from the belief in a being (i.e. in something that one believes to be real), and the belief that humans can elicit the help and assistance of these beings for their concerns."[61]

Humans are looking for help and to lead lives that are balanced, fulfilling and satisfying in all respects. The whole world is looking for help. The cry for help is universal. In his Letter to the Romans (8:22-23), Paul puts it as follows: "For we know that the whole creation groans and travails in pain together until now. And not only they, but ourselves also, which have the first fruits of the Spirit, even we ourselves groan within ourselves, waiting for the adoption, to wit, the redemption of our body."

---

[61] Op. cit., p. 320. – 'Magie rechnet in genau der gleichen Weise mit übernatürlichen Mächten, wie 'Religion' es tut. Beide haben ihre Wurzeln in der überirdischen Welt. 'Magie' und 'Religion' gehen von dergleichen Grundlage aus, nämlich vom Glauben an ein Wesen (d.h. an etwas, das er für real hält), und daran, daß der Mensch von diesem Wesen Hilfe und Beistand für seine Belange bekommen kann.'

Behind Paul's cry for redemption lies an obligatory "must". Humans must cry out, for they are depraved. Their cry for help and redemption hails from their depravity. They have squandered the chance to live a good and proper life. Their cry for redemption is therefore justified, since they know that their life could be so much better. They have a very good idea of how things should actually be. But since things are not as humans imagine that they should be, they feel empty and unfulfilled. They feel a deep longing for the lost gifts of unity. Humans have only themselves to blame for the fact that their reality looks rather different from what they imagine it to be. Nobody but they themselves are responsible for the mistakes they made. No spirit, no being, no deity has led them to be tempted to live a different kind of life as they were originally meant to live. Humans themselves have chosen to change the way they live; it is what they wanted. They did however not envisage the fatal consequences their decision to live a different life would have. The gamble they took in order to acquire a greater amount of wisdom and insight did not pay off. They were punished for their act of wanting to know more. One side of their existence, the good side, was familiar to them; that was apparently not enough. They decided to gain control of the other side as well. This other side of their life has proven to be to their own detriment: after the Fall, related in Genesis 3, humans were introduced to evil. The decision had been left up to them. It lay in their discretion to do what God had commanded: "Thou shalt not eat …" In a purportedly unobserved moment, with their own perception of things and out of their own free will, humans turned away from God. The Bible calls this act of disobedience sin. God's first commandment did not fall on obedient, fertile ground. Humans overreached their freedom, misusing it towards their God. They acted with iniquity, an iniquity that is held against them. They cannot exonerate themselves from this iniquity. It adheres to them; they have turned into sinners. The cause of all evil in the world is the disobedience of humans in not heeding the very first commandment given to them by God.

After humans had succumbed to the first temptation, others soon arose that they could not resist either. Humans are continuously being led into temptation. And, time and again, they have given in to these temptations. Over and above these human temptations, and due to God's understanding of humans, a totally different kind of temptation occurred into which God entered personally: the temptation of his Son. Jesus was tempted by the devil before he could embark on his divine mission. Jesus experienced a temptation similar to those that other people have been faced with throughout history. A number of monks who sought to live a reclusive life had to endure many hours of horror, as they were surrounded and tempted by many evil spirits.

Once again I submit a personal example: I have forgotten what time or year it was. I must have been around twenty years old. I was a young man looking for answers and my religious doubts had reached crisis point. My faith had begun to unravel. All imperatives and good intentions began to fail. The burning questions: Where is God? Does he actually exist or is he pure invention? Can I find him? began to give rise to profound feelings of doubt about his existence and power. One evening, during my contemplations, I felt myself slipping into an unconscious state. I was physically healthy. There was really not much wrong with me. During that state of unconsciousness my life passed before my eyes like a movie. Beautiful landscapes appeared, something that I watched with pleasure. Nevertheless, I couldn't shake off a sense of unease as I continued watching. I wanted to rid myself of these images but was unable to do so. So, in this rather unnatural and strange state I decided to turn to God, which I succeeded to do. When I called upon the Lord to help me, he helped me. After I had concluded my prayer in that visionary state I woke up. During the next 14 days my faith was so strong that I could have "moved mountains", to use a Biblical expression. I wished that my faith would always remain that strong.

I will accept a psychological explanation of what I had experienced: "The unconscious mind took up the pressing questions of the conscious mind and assumed control when the patient was no longer able to answer these questions himself. It initiated the vision to seek a solution to the problem and effect a harmonious state between the unconscious and conscious mind." But I think I can also say that God acted beyond these psychological explanations, or maybe even through them. I personally like to speak of God's guidance in this incident. I see the course of events in relation to my faith. In doing so, I am not trying to dismiss the questions that visions pose as being irrelevant. But I assimilate that which has happened to me into my life as a Christian.

The temptation of Jesus (Matt 4:1-11) occurs at the beginning of his ministry. It is significant that the Lord is first subjected to a great temptation before he can embark on his heavenly mission on earth. All three temptations test his faith and the obedience it entails. Jesus is not asked to provide proof of his divinity for his mission, nor to demonstrate his power. He emphasises his relationship with and love for his father: in all three replies he refers his tempter to the First Commandment. Before he even starts his ministry, the tempter dares him to abuse the powers of his divine origin just this once. Is it really that serious if one breaks God's commandments just once? But he takes this provocation very seriously. For him, everything is at stake, his entire mission and his position as the Son of God. He does not yield to the temptation in any way. He invokes Scripture, seeks mercy's will therein and gives praise to God alone. The three words of Scripture that Jesus cites: "Man does not live by bread alone, but man lives by every word that comes from the mouth of the LORD" (Deut 8:3), "You shall not put the LORD your God to the test" (Deut 6:16) and "It is the LORD your God you shall fear. Him you shall serve" (Deut 6:13) have become a source of comfort and help to many people during their own episodes of temptation or similar situations. The author of the Letter to the Hebrews (4:15b) strikes a sympathetic note when he writes: We have a Lord "who in every respect has been tempted as we are, yet without sin."

Every temptation contains within it a decision; a decision that can be made in one of two ways. The tempter can either come into his or her own if the person that is being tempted does not object; or the person that is being tempted can reject the tempter by resisting him or her. There is no middle ground.

There are always forces at play where religious temptations are concerned. A battle ensues. However, the conflict does not so much take place between the two opposing forces of good and evil; the battle is decided between the tempter and the person in the middle, as it were, who has been marked out for the battle. The place where this battle is carried out is the human being, and his or her soul. The tempter represents one side, human beings the other. It is a spiritual battle which may, in the event of a person's indecision, extend to involve the body or the material world. The decision for one side or the other lies with humans themselves. They can and have to decide. In doing so, the environment that had a formative influence on them may well be a contributing factor, but the individual nonetheless assumes responsibility for his or her decision.

In a society that operates along collective thought structures, this principle also holds true. There, too, the human takes centre stage. It is not the person in the middle who decides the outcome of the battle, however, but the powers of good and evil. It is a one-sided battle. One of the two forces will fight its way to the fore. Humans find themselves under the spell of these forces. If they resist these forces, as is often the case, the same battle will ensue. The end result is that either humans prevail, or else the powers emerge triumphant. In many cases the good or evil force wins, in most instances it is the good force that prevails. According to the understanding of the *Batswana*, these good forces are the spirits of their benevolent ancestors.

In the temptation of Christ, it initially seems as if the battle might end badly. At least that may be assumed at first. Jesus gives an answer to each of the three temptations. This in itself is extraordinary. He talks to his tempter. Within the understanding of the collective, there is probably no example in existence showing that it is possible for someone who is being tempted by the spirits to actually talk to them. When the ancestral spirits pay a person a visit, that person remains a silent recipient of that vision.

By citing Old-Testament verses, Jesus intimates that he knows the Bible very well. Each quotation outdoes the one proffered by his tempter. It transpires that Jesus' knowledge of the Scriptures is vastly superior to that of his adversary. But it is not his sustained superiority, wisdom or ability that results in him being hailed, or that he – as might retrospectively be assumed – was carried through because he is the Son of God; he prevailed through simple obedience towards his heavenly Father. Jesus is tempted as a human being, not as a divine one. His temptation is of a human nature. That is why it is plausible and comprehensible. And that is why it could also easily have turned out differently. Be that as it may, one should nevertheless keep open the possibility that the outcome of the temptation was not a fore-gone conclusion.

When Jesus was tempted he was able to resist the devil. Because of his temptation, God was also drawn into the situation. The verdict on Jesus' position – ambivalent and difficult to grasp – that he is truly God and truly man at the same time was rendered at the First Council of Nicaea. A verdict that has embroiled the history of the Church in disputes ever since. But precisely therein lies the profound mystery of the Christian faith: that he became fully human while remaining fully divine. One is unable to fully grasp the extent of what God has done through him. But one can accept and believe that which one is unable to understand. And one is able to train one's faith in the Lord of heaven and earth. By training one's faith, it becomes a part of everyday life. And by practising their faith, Christians give glory to the Lord their God.

So when Christians in Europe read the story of Jesus' temptations, do they understand and interpret it in the same way that Christians in Africa do? The Christians in Africa are likely to have a different understanding of it than the Christians in Europe. The African Christians possibly even understand it better than their European counterparts. Why may one reach this conclusion? If it can be assumed that Satan operates by way of sorcerous means, that everything that is genuinely satanic may be traced back to an origin of sorcery, then the temptations of Jesus are pervaded by sorcerous satanic practises. One can imagine that God could in all possibility have turned stones into loaves of bread, as Satan was demanding. It would, in any event, seem to be a small miracle for God to perform. One can equally imagine that God's angels would have been able to catch Jesus if he should have thrown himself from the pinnacle of the temple. After having been directly addressed and challenged by Satan to kneel before him, however, it would be very difficult to imagine that Jesus would have believed in him and worshipped him.

Two fundamentally different forces collide with one another: the power of God which has, for the moment, seemingly been pushed into the background but which is still discernible in the fact that Jesus pledges total dedication and obedience to God's will and power; and Satan who, with evil intent, blatantly brings his magical powers into play in front of Jesus' eyes. In his understanding, stones can be transformed by magical means, something the satanic magical power has demonstrated often enough by way of numerous examples. In his understanding, a person who has attracted these satanic magical powers can furthermore fly through the air, something that can also be verified by numerous examples. Thirdly, there are a number of people who worship Satan and are therefore under his occult spell. All three temptations form part of Satan's reality. People engage with Satan's temptations, and many are taken in by them. Jesus let Satan come close to him, something we humans should not necessarily do, seeing that we have our free will to stay away from evil and sorcery, and to reject them. I have become wiser after my experiences, but also more mature.

Jesus' freedom to choose was also put to the test. He did not fall for the enticingly seductive traps set for him by Satan. By letting himself be approached by Satan's temptations, Jesus encountered a totally different kind of power, the satanic magical power, and in quite an extreme manner. He comes into contact with sorcery right at the beginning of his ministry and, upon encountering it, he rejects and repels it. While he rejects it with the first two temptations, he intensifies his rejection of Satan in the third temptation. He repels him in a radical manner. He addresses him and says: "Away from me, Satan!" John (1:14) says: "And the Word became flesh and dwelt among us." We may gather from this text that Jesus was familiar with all aspects of life. The world of magic and sorcery is one such aspect, which can pollute and destroy one's spirit and body.

If Africa still holds on to a magical world view, the Christians in Africa probably appreciate the temptation story on a deeper and more intense level. In his article: "*Gibt es Zauberhandlungen*?" (Do acts of magic exist?), A. Jensen takes up the story of Jesus' temptation. He compares magic to religion, stating the following: "But in what way magic stands outside the religious sphere and finds itself, for the most part, to be its exact opposite, is illustrated with unparalleled clarity in the New Testament account of what is called the Temptation of Christ. It speaks of the power that subjugates gods and humans, the power that is the most salient feature of all genuine magical acts. With the religious founder's brusquely hostile rejection ('Away from me, Satan!') we sense the unbridgeable chasm between magic and religion. But we also learn something else with equal clarity: If Christ is tempted to transform stones into loaves of bread or to float down from the roof of a temple, he must have felt the capability to do so within himself."[62]

Satan tempted Jesus, the Son of God, by means of his magical capabilities. Jesus accepted the temptation. Satan, the sorcerer, summoned up various experiments. He utilised all the powers at his disposal. Jesus did not succumb to Satan's temptations, which would have led to a falling away from God and great sin.

With the temptation of Jesus, God was led into temptation also. Ever since Genesis 3 it is Satan's perpetually recurring desire to tempt God. He knows that he cannot deceive him but that doesn't stop him from trying. The desire to tempt God lies behind all sorcerous acts, all witchcraft and utilisation of magical powers. To tempt God is an act of wrongdoing. Humans distance themselves from God if they let themselves succumb to the allures of Satan. They sin against God, Christ and the Holy Spirit if they abandon their status as being children of God and succumb to other powers. Thanks be to God that Jesus accepted and prevailed over all temptations. Thanks be to God that Jesus has cleared the way to the Father. And, thanks be to God that we may believe in Jesus Christ as the Lord of heaven and earth, as our Lord, who is at our side when temptations arise. Jesus has deepened the faith in God within us. Jesus presented us with a new kind of faith, a faith that cannot be compared with that of any other religion. He lived his faith as an example to the world. In every situation he strove to be one with the Father and to do His will; he was

---

[62] Op. cit., p. 289. 'In welcher Weise aber das Magische außerhalb der religiösen Sphäre steht, meist ihr gerade entgegengesetzt ist, zeigt sich mit einmaliger Deutlichkeit an jenem Bericht des Neuen Testaments, der die Versuchung Christi genannt wird. Hier ist von der Götter und Menschen bezwingenden Macht die Rede, die das hervorstechendste Merkmal aller echt magischen Handlungen ist. Wir spüren an der schroff feindseligen Ablehnung des Religionsstifters ("Hebe dich weg von mir, Satan!") die unüberbrückbare Kluft zwischen der Magie und der Religion. Wir erfahren aber noch etwas anderes mit gleicher Deutlichkeit: Wenn Christus in Versuchung gerät, Steine in Brot zu verwandeln oder von dem Dach eines Tempels herab zu schweben, so muß er doch wohl die Fähigkeit dazu in sich verspürt haben.'

faithful and obedient as no other before or after him. The Son was totally devoted to the Father and adhered to His promises. The New Testament gives an account of him being the one Lord who recognised the truth. It is for this reason that the New Testament points only to him, and it is up to us to look up to him, to worship and follow him. Jesus had faith in his Father. He had a faith that cannot be surpassed, neither can it be compared to the faith of any other founder of religion. It is possible, in view of the "Messiah mystery" of Jesus that is shimmering through the gospels of Mark and John, that Jesus was affected and supported in the depths of his soul by the faith that exists in the celestial world among the angels and heavenly hosts. The angels were close to him (Matt 4:11). They watched his temptation. After Jesus had repelled Satan and his magical powers, the angels sympathised with him, strengthening him in the way that was familiar to both of them, in heavenly, good, everlasting divine faith.

Jesus has broken the magical power of Satan for the Christians in Africa, and for all people who have come into contact with the powers of evil. He has not annihilated evil. It continues to exist and is capable of wreaking great havoc. Neither has Jesus launched an appeal to fight against evil in his name. Evil must at all times be taken into account. But the power that evil wields has been weakened.

Even though Jesus conquered evil, it has not been obliterated. Jesus can intervene and help when evil erupts. Whoever believes in him will witness miracles in themselves and the world around them. But faith does not guarantee miracles. That is why there will always be Christians who become disillusioned with the Christian faith; it doesn't deliver the miracles they had envisioned. Even so, if these Christians are supported by their belief in forgiveness and eternal life, and have to endure the manifestations of evil for a shorter or longer period of time and accept that, if, for example, there exists only a small margin – as far as is humanly possible to tell – for a successful healing to take place, then that constitutes a small miracle in itself. Even in a seemingly hopeless situation, one's trust in the mercy and grace of God should be rated higher than the negative confession of having failed during a specific point in one's life. When Jesus was about to start his ministry, he was not only tempted once, but several times. He wasn't found lacking once. That elevates him to the

Lord of all of God's world. Jesus was, is and remains the Lord. He was, is and remains the "Lord of all".

The Bible speaks of evil in different ways. It is aware of the magical powers and the sorcery committed by the pagan tribes around Israel. The most well-known narratives in this regard are the "Witch of Endor" (1 Sam 28:7-12) and "Simon the Sorcerer" (Acts 8:9-11). The Bible also speaks of the evil thoughts that originate in the human heart (Mk 7:21-23), of cosmic evil spirits (Eph 6:12), as well as of evil and Satan many, many times. There is no denying, in view of things being so dark worldwide, that the coming of Jesus has something to do with the power of evil. Perhaps this sinful, evil world is the only reason why Jesus was compelled to exchange his heavenly life with life on this earth. H. Haag states: "Jesus' life and death can only be comprehended in its entirety against the background of evil."[63]

Jesus Christ, the Son sent by the Father, remained true to his heavenly faith. He has revealed his faith to all people who believe in God through him and the Holy Spirit. The trust that exists in the heavenly communion of God is bestowed in the church on the faithful through the presence of Christ. Jesus is the core of faith. Whoever believes in him and lets him- or herself consistently be drawn towards him, will receive the inviting promise of heavenly faith in eternal communion with God. Jesus alone ensures my faith. It is in him that trust and life can be found, promising something very good.

The Christians among the *Batswana* don't only pray to Jesus as their Lord and God. They can also accept him as their new friend, superior or king. He understood his mission and executed it to the satisfaction of all. We can trust in him. A Passion hymn in the Lutheran hymnal (89:1) addresses and celebrates Jesus' faith. It reads: „*Jesus glaube sehr/tüchtig, denn du hast mich ja geliebt! Mein Herz ist ganz bei dir, denn du bist für uns gestorben."* (*Jesu o dumele thata, wena yo o nthatileng! Pelo ya me ea go rata, wena yo o re swetseng* = Jesus, be strong in faith, for it is you who loved me! I give my heart to you, for you have died for us). The Christians among the *Batswana* have comprehended that, compared to Jesus, the faith in which they live

---

[63] Op. cit., p. 266. – 'Das ganze Leben und Sterben Jesu wird nur begreifbar vor dem Hintergrund des Bösen.'

their lives is but a small one, whereas Jesus demonstrates the abso-
lute faith. That is why they, together with other Christians, turn to
Jesus who acts with a strong faith that enables him to overcome all
evil and darkness in the world. Jesus acted with an "entirely different" faith, a new, strong faith that has the power to supersede evil
and the power of magic. Hymn 91:6b: *"Jesu geh' voran ... Wir folgen
deinem Glauben ... In Worten und in der Tat werde ich dir leben, Herr,
durch die Kraft des Glaubens"* (*Mo mafokong le mo tirong ke tla phe-
lela wena, Mong, ka thata ya tumelo* = Jesus, still lead on ... We follow your faith ... In word and in deed I will live for you, Lord, by the
power of faith).

That the *Batswana*, and Africans generally, attach great importance
to the historical Jesus may have to do with the fact that they lay
greater emphasis on past and present tenses. The linear thinking of
the Judaeo-Christian belief system emphasises all three tenses,
whereas the African traditional religion points more towards the experiences of the past and the realities of the present. J.S. Mbiti
states: "African concepts of time lay greater emphasis on the past
and present than on the future, making the future virtually non-
existent beyond a few months or years."[64] If this conception of time
holds true for Africa, the old belief system and culture of the *Batswana* have had an influence on their adopted Christian belief. As a
consequence, the first missionaries did not translate the German
hymns literally in this instance, transferring them from one culture to
the other; they were adapted to the African context and translated
correctly.

Every Christian has his or her own story of faith. Every Christian has
to prove him- or herself, the faith that has been bestowed on them
has to prove itself. All Christians encounter afflictions of faith, and
they turn out differently for each person. Nobody is exempt from the
temptations of the devil. No-one has the same afflictions as someone
else. Through these afflictions, faith escapes from its confines into
the breadth and width of the mystery of Christ. Faith in Jesus Christ
entails all kinds of afflictions and temptations. If Christians accept
these afflictions of faith and subsequently rise above them, they can

---

[64] Op. cit., p. 12.

regard them as having been a gift. They bring Christians closer to God and make a better person out of them.

Temptations and afflictions are a part of the Christian faith. They appertain to faith and attest to it. What would the result be if one's faith could be turned into a fixed component in one's life as a Christian? Would we not then act in a rather arrogant, disdainful way towards others if it were in our hands that our faith, our imperatives and services assured a good outcome to our life on earth and an eternal life hereafter? We may hope and have faith that all this will be so, but the ultimate certainty that everything will turn out the way we imagine it, that all will be well, lies solely in the trust we put in God our Lord.

Times of temptation and affliction of faith lead to the insight that one's religious life has evolved beyond the initial stage and is being put to the test. Doubts may arise during such times as to the veracity of the beliefs one adopted as a Christian in one's early days, and what one fought for when one initially had certainty of faith, or what one professed towards others.

During an affliction of faith Christians can experience great uncertainty about what it is that they believe. If they can accept this affliction, however, and can come through it and refrain from taking a decision of their own accord against the faith that was bestowed on them, the Lord will lead them into a guided faith, guidance being the more important path of faith. In the Lord's Prayer it says: "Your will be done on earth as it is in heaven." Afflictions of faith are quintessentially God's will: The Lord leads us into them and helps us to overcome them. God knows about them; he willed them. He allows them. They form part of those little temptations that are unavoidable for an advanced life in faith.

Afflictions of faith, and the uncertainty accompanying them, do not diminish one's faith. They lead one past what lies on the surface into the depth; a depth that conceals something sinister on the one hand, but which also always comprises something good on the other. Faith is something good. Afflictions of faith are something good. God is good, and the humans he created are also good. "And God saw everything that he had made, and behold, it was very good." (Gen 1:31)

But faith comprises more than that which is good. It directs one's senses towards the Lord of heaven and earth. Faith does not guarantee the deliverance from evil, to be sure, but it implies it. The believer is delivered from sin and death. Through the faith in Jesus Christ, God has offered the believer a promise to grant him or her a life after death.

5. Life after death

The question as to whether there is life after death has occupied humans throughout the ages and all over the world. All religions and even Communism, which never intended to be a religion at all, ask the question whether there exists an afterlife. The different religions provide diverging answers. All religions leave no doubt about the fact that life on this earth indeed ends with death. Even though many people nowadays don't concern themselves with the question of life in the hereafter, due either to indifference or broad-mindedness, this question continues to be taken up by the various religions and is affirmed by all spiritual people.

In the concluding part of this book, we align ourselves with those religions and spiritual people who profess the belief in a life that continues after physical death has occurred; but we also differentiate ourselves from them. Our conception of an afterlife conforms to that of the apostle Paul. We embrace his conception, which he describes in the first letter to the Corinthians. The various religions, sects and movements have developed their own conceptions in this regard with the help of dreams, visions, apparitions and other clever ideas.

The question we first have to ask, however, is: Is there any evidence that life continues after death? On the one hand no human being has ever seen the hereafter. On the other hand, there are a number of suppositions that point towards an existence of life after death.

Quite a number of people, due to their experiences with supernatural forces or because they have had near-death experiences during which the so-called portal to the Great Beyond was subsequently opened in their mind's eye, are convinced that there exists an afterlife. In that case the question as to whether there is life after death is no longer a subject of debate. It simply exists.

Many people among the *Batswana* are convinced that their deceased fathers and mothers still live on. They have seen them in diurnal visions. But instances where the ancestors appear to them in a dream at night are more frequent. People who have seen or experienced their ancestors in a dream do not doubt the existence of ancestral spirits. According to the traditional belief of the *Batswana*, death constitutes the transition into the ancestral community and collective.

Spiritism could possibly also provide evidence. In Namibia, the only daughter of a nine-person family of German aristocratic descent dies during the time of attending confirmation classes. The parents are totally devastated for a long time. They only find peace after a spiritist, in her specific way, summons their daughter from an otherworld, who then tells her parents that she lives in peace with God. The parents are convinced that their daughter is at peace in God's hands. For them, the encounter with their deceased daughter is proof that there is life after death.

Esotericism, which is favourably disposed towards the spirits of the past and which, together with the famous Goethe, Steiner, Swedenborg and others, incorporates such experiences into its religion, believes that spirit apparitions provide just as much proof as is provided by the individual person whose mother-in-law, uncle or spouse appears before his or her inner eye sometime after their death, or appears standing next to them and talking to them. Hardly any more evidence seems to be required when the person who has returned from the grave subsequently addresses the person chosen by them, conveying their wishes or imparting sympathetic communications for the living.

We gather from a quote by R. Hummel that there are six different ways in which the assumption of an afterlife may possibly be proven. Hummel himself does not hold this view. He writes: "After having suffered an accident or some other health crisis during which [individuals] have returned from near-death experiences, they report seeing visions of light in line with the motto: 'I was clinically dead' (1), experiencing apparitions of deceased people (2), as well as soul journeys (3) to hitherto unknown places. Were they really in 'the beyond', bringing back news to the land of the living? This follows the same line as the new and rekindled interest in similar experiences from earlier religious history: in shamanistic ecstasies (the shaman being the medicine man in Setswana) (4) and practises related to them, in meditative out-of-body experiences (5) as well as in drug-induced states of consciousness (6)."[65] All six of these possibilities are accompanied by examples that point to the fact that an afterlife cannot only be assumed; these examples are already proof in itself of its existence.

Parapsychologists, who record cases of spirit apparitions and carry out investigations into them, differ in how they assess these incidents that encroach on this world from an unknown otherworld. One question that occupies parapsychologists is the following: Does the apparition emanate from a deceased human being, or is it prompted and attracted in some way by a living person, or does the apparition constitute an autonomous phenomenon which emanates and sends its transmissions from an extra-terrestrial place "elsewhere"? Some parapsychological researchers, who concern themselves exclusively with spirits in this fairly recently established science, consider them to be living entities. One incident is known to have occurred in Britain: Two friends agreed that, whoever died first would come back and manifest himself to the other. The encounter took place, as per agreement, three weeks after the death of one of the two friends.

Radical parapsychologists oppose the assumption that spirits are alive. They claim that all manifestations constitute an intrapersonal problem which can, in the final analysis, be ascribed to the common denominator "psi" (psyche/soul). Only in the event that the deeper layers of the individual and collective soul could be probed and re-

---

[65] Op. cit., p. 14. – 'Nach einem Unfall oder einer gesundheitlichen Krise aus dem Grenzbereich des Todes wieder zurückgekehrt, berichten sie nach dem Motto 'Ich war klinisch tot' über Lichtvisionen (1), Erscheinungen Verstorbener (2) und Seelenreisen (3) in bislang unbekannte Räume. Waren sie wirklich 'drüben' und bringen Kunde zurück in das Land der Lebenden? Auf der gleichen Linie liegt das neu erwachte Interesse an vergleichbaren Erfahrungen aus der früheren Religionsgeschichte: an schamanistischen (Schamane ist im *Setswana* der Medizinmann) Ekstasen (4) und den dazu gehörenden Praktiken, an meditativen Entrückungen (5) und drogen¬induzierten Bewußtseinszuständen (6).'

searched more thoroughly will the issue of spirit apparitions be resolved.

Are those psychologists and parapsychologists correct who claim that all apparitions of dead people on all levels are psychologically induced? Nobody knows for sure, of course. Arguments can be brought forward either way, no matter how many attempts are made concerning spirit apparitions. Each person can propound their own position on the matter. To date, no researcher has been able to provide irrefutable proof concerning the apparitions of spirits and present findings convincing everybody of their veracity. One is compelled to grant these researchers of the spirit world one thing, though: time and again, it is humans who are central to all these kinds of events, and not spirits. Humans call on the spirits because they want to glean information from them. They summon them because things have become too boring or too uncomfortable in the social environment in which they find themselves. In an attempt to reach for the stars in an exotic way or to desperately come up with a final solution to a problem, humans give the spirit world a try.

In other cases, yet again, when the spirit power makes itself known as such, humans will not reject it but heed the message of the spirits and pass it on. It remains an open question as to whether humans themselves once produced these spirits with their mind and will, with their fears and resentments, and continue to do so; and whether they are now deluding themselves as to their existence or whether these spirits have indeed invaded our reality from a world other than the human one. In other words: spirits inhabit their own world. They are summoned by humans. They exist as good and evil spirits mainly because they present themselves as being the spirits of the deceased who seek a continual relationship with the living.

Spirit manifestations are a reality. There is no doubt about that. For the most part, they make their appearances where a magical world view continues to inform the collective belief system. They appear elsewhere when individuals from lower levels of society live according to their own beliefs. They also appear when they are sought out and approached by people from the most diverse backgrounds, upbringing and levels of education. In most cases they are attracted from within a person's conscious or unconscious sphere. Humans will pursue them consciously if they no longer feel comfortable in their familiar surroundings, are ready to take a risk, i.e. wish to outdo others, or if they were initially introduced to the spirit world in an uncomplicated manner and are, due to an altered state of inner longing, subsequently compelled to seek them out again and again.

We are still searching for an answer to the question: Is there evidence of life after death? We could, at this point, agree with all those religious people to whom the spirits have manifested as a reality through the ancestors, esoteric and spiritistic practises, or also through the study of parapsychology. Many of those people who have had an encounter with spirits need no further proof other than their own experience. They are very sure about their encounter with the spirit world. For them, their experience is proof that there is an afterlife. All further considerations consequently become invalid. This group of people attracts followers who embrace their testimony.

If spirits do indeed exist that operate outside the Church, it should come as no surprise that there are other spirits who insinuate themselves into the Church. This is indeed so. There seem to be different ways of life after death. This so-called evidence of an afterlife is most frequently observed in the Catholic Church. Faith in the Catholic Church is constructed on a broad, expansive basis which extends beyond the Gospels. The inquiry as to what else may be incorporated into the Christian faith lies with the hierarchy of the church. There is no doubt in the minds of believers as to the apparitions of Christ, the Virgin Mary and various Saints; the Catholic church further endorses these by organising pilgrimages to the apparition sites, thereby providing double evidence of an afterlife. Catholic believers view these apparitions as being absolutely real and the Catholic church concurs. In the 20th century alone the apparitions of the Virgin Mary – according to the statistics of the Catholic church – are said to have been over 600.[66]

---

[66] The question that needs to be asked is: Why does the Virgin Mary appear only to those of the Catholic faith? Do the apparitions of the mother of Jesus constitute a latter-day revelation of God, or are they the product of the teachings and dogma of the Catholic church?

It is all too human and also understandable that a spiritual person should seek evidence for what they believe in. And, if someone is looking for evidence, they will find it. Hence nobody can argue with them over that. Is the search for proof reconcilable with the will of God? The Bible not only disapproves of the search for proof but also prohibits believers from consulting the spirits or seeking some kind of fellowship with them in order to satisfy their own human wishes and desires.

In the first of the Ten Commandments, our heavenly Father lays claim to absoluteness, to be worshipped to the exclusion of all others. The Lord tolerates no other spirits before Him. The Israelites were obliged to receive this unequivocal and harsh declaration thousands of years ago already. The people of Israel most radically rejected sorcerers (Ex 22:17) and necromancers (Lev 20:17). King Saul reiterates the prohibition against the spiritists and diviners of his time. But when he himself suffers great distress on one occasion, he seeks the counsel of a woman who is a necromancer (1 Sam 28), whereupon he is struck by God's wrath. There are many people who behave very much like Saul. If something in their lives has unsettled them or they are facing great suffering, they seek comfort outside the Christian faith.[67]

In the Semitic world view of ancient Israel, which bears resemblance to a number of related characteristics of the collective cultural life of the Batswana, the living and the dead are strongly interconnected. The dead return to their forefathers. At the same time the ancestors assist the living. Serving as an outward sign of the connection between the two worlds, the working implements of the deceased are placed into the grave with them, as in Eze 32:27, for instance, where the fallen heroes are buried with their weapons. And Samuel was buried in the robe he wore as a prophet (1 Sam 28:3.13-14). This conviction, dating from Israel's early history and resembling that of

---

[67] I met a woman called Jane recently. After the rather sudden death of her first husband, she had consulted a fortune-teller in Cape Town. In spite of her profound feelings of grief she was nonetheless not prepared to have the fortune-teller summon her husband. After her second husband also died in a tragic accident, I encountered her at a Christian retreat and recreational facility where she had come to be quiet and pray.

Batswana traditional belief, could be added to the possible proof listed above. There appears to be adequate evidence of an afterlife.

The New Testament incorporates this belief that originated from a native region of Israel, does however reject the notion of evidence of faith in the same way that Moses and the prophets did earlier. The New Testament departs from the notion of a collective faith and places humans before God as individuals. Through the Son of God, and transcending the collective and all and any cultural way of thinking, the individual person is presented with a new community of Christians.

There lies a long journey between Abraham and Christ. Many changes have occurred during the course of God's history; yet there are other things that hardly ever change. Let us cast our minds back to Saul once more and compare the manifestation of Samuel with one of Jesus' manifestations. Saul goes to see the spiritist of Endor. He is greatly alarmed after Samuel's spirit spoke to him. While Saul is scared to death after Samuel's judgement of him, Jesus' disciples, too, take great fright at the appearance of a spirit. They initially think that they are seeing a ghost and then, when the phenomenon takes shape, they see Jesus coming towards them over the lake. (Mk 6:45-49). The fact that the disciples think that they are seeing a ghost even though it is the Lord, means that they must have been familiar with or even have experienced many different ghost stories. Ghost and spirit manifestations are a familiar concept to King Saul and Jesus' disciples. In Saul's case a spiritist summons the ghost of Samuel from an otherworld, while it may be assumed in the case of the disciples that the spirits, for their part, are able to appear by way of a manifestation.

Another occurrence related in the New Testament gives us particular cause to reflect on the probability of an afterlife. But first, we pose the questions that people of all time have continually asked, and to which we are only able to supply parts of an answer, for example: Where do the deceased go after death? Is there a specific place for them? Are they living with God? Are bad people turned away, and good people accepted? Will reconciliation eventually occur for all humans, after a certain period of time and in a certain place? A full explanation to these and similar questions is still outstanding. And to speculate on these matters is not worth it. Our heavenly Father has reserved the exclusive domain to provide final answers to these questions for another time.

The one story in the Bible that astounds us, that poses many questions upon closer inspection, that gives esotericism and the New Age movement occasion to align themselves with Christianity and that must, in its final analysis, be ascribed to the mystery of God and assigned to the Christian faith, is written in Mk 9:2-10. This beautiful narrative reads as follows: "And after six days Jesus took with him Peter and James and John, and led them up a high mountain by themselves. And he was transfigured before them, and his clothes became radiant, intensely white, as no one on earth could bleach them. And there appeared to them Elijah with Moses, and they were talking with Jesus. And Peter said to Jesus, 'Rabbi, it is good that we are here. Let us make three tents, one for you and one for Moses and one for Elijah.' For he did not know what to say, for they were terrified. And a cloud overshadowed them, and a voice came out of the cloud, 'This is my beloved Son; listen to him.' And suddenly, looking around, they no longer saw anyone with them but Jesus only. And as they were coming down the mountain, he charged them to tell no one what they had seen, until the Son of Man had risen from the dead. So they kept the matter to themselves, questioning what this rising from the dead might mean."

It is better to open oneself up and take in this Bible story than to talk or hold a sermon about it. In my assessment this is a beautiful text, challenging us to meditate on it. At the end of the "Transfiguration of Jesus" the disciples ask: "What does rising from the dead mean?" Up to that point and for various reasons this had not been a burning question for them. The Jewish faith did not place an emphasis on life after death, but on obedience to God and His commandments.

In the Christian faith, at the end of a journey filled with promise, lies the resurrection.

Beyond all the messages, the miracles and the cross of Jesus, the resurrection constitutes the ultimate great consolation in a Christian's life, a consolation which has no comparison in any other religion. In the Bible itself, at the end of each gospel, the highlight of the resurrection is underscored as being the culmination of Christ's victory over death. The evangelists describe various encounters with the resurrected Lord. In one of these resurrection stories an account is given of a clarifying conversation that took place between Jesus and his disciples. Unfortunately, far too little attention is paid to it in the church and especially in African churches, and in places where the spirits continue to play a major role in people's lives. It apparently finds itself on the peripheries rather than at the centre of Christian proclamation. And yet it contains an important message that extends far beyond the straightforward faith in the resurrection. It is worth quoting this text from Lk 24:33-43 here as well: "And they rose that same hour and returned to Jerusalem. And they found the eleven and those who were with them gathered together, saying, 'The Lord has risen indeed, and has appeared to Simon!' Then they told what had happened on the road, and how he was known to them in the breaking of the bread. As they were talking about these things, Jesus himself stood among them, and said to them, 'Peace be with you!' But they were startled and frightened and thought they saw a spirit. And he said to them, 'Why are you troubled, and why do doubts arise in your hearts? See my hands and my feet, that it is I myself. Touch me, and see. For a spirit does not have flesh and bones as you see that I have.' And when he had said this, he showed them his hands and his feet. And while they still disbelieved for joy and were marvelling, he said to them, 'Have you anything here to eat?' They gave him a piece of broiled fish, and he took it and ate before them."

Belief in the resurrection tells us, first and foremost, that Jesus, the Son of God, has been proclaimed as God's Christ. He has rendered death harmless. He transformed the uncertainty of his disciples as to his whereabouts into joy. The words he uses to reveal himself to his disciples: "Don't be afraid!" and "Peace be with you!" are among the words that are most frequently passed on by the Church. If one should summarise the message of the New Testament, the resurrection can be compared to the dot on the letter "i". Without this crucial little dot on the vowel "i" it would cease to be a letter and become a vacuous line, deriving its meaning from elsewhere.

According to the evangelist Luke, the above-mentioned conversation did take place, even though the other evangelists do not describe it in quite the same amount of detail. But they were all present. Mark (16:14) as well as John (20:19-20) confirm the conversation. Something else in the words the Lord spoke to them has become important to these two evangelists as they experienced the exciting moment of their Lord's apparition. In spite of the excitement of the moment it was Luke who probably paid the closest attention. Mark and John indicate in their gospels that they concur with Luke's rendition of the event. Apart from conveying the general message of the resurrection, Luke emphasises an aspect that is widely known but is, at the same time, addressed with some awkwardness and reluctance in public. The other disciples decline to talk or write about it. It is only Luke who points out the critical issue that Jesus picks up from their reaction upon seeing him. They all fall silent. Nobody utters a word. They are all thinking the same thing. The way he suddenly appears, unannounced and through closed doors, can, in their human understanding of such matters, only be reconciled with ghost hauntings and spirits. "But they were startled and frightened and thought they saw a spirit. And he said to them, 'Why are you troubled, and why do doubts arise in your hearts?'"

Jesus makes two important statements, reassuring them that he is not a ghost and telling them how he is different from a spirit. He shows them his physical body and asks them to touch him. No ghost or spirit has ever managed to transform itself to the degree that the Lord has been able to do. Accordingly, he says: "For a spirit does not have flesh and bones as you see that I have." When the disciples continue to be startled and are not sure what to make of the apparition, the Lord continues to minister to them in order to turn their shock into trust. He asks them for something to eat. This, too, is not the behaviour of a spirit during an apparition. A spirit conjures up things or makes them disappear. There is certainly no knowledge of a spirit ever having asked for food. At best, spirits can swop, carry off or spoil food but they never behave in a way where they eat in front of other people. The disciples obey and give Jesus some of their fried fish, which was lying on the table in front of them during the meal. The risen Lord eats and they recognise him at last.

Since his appearance between Easter and Ascension, Christ has not made another appearance for the last 2,000 years or so. He will return at a time that God has ordained for his second coming (Mk 13:26.31-32). The spirits, on the other hand, continue to operate. They come and go as they please. The spirits are not known to have imparted a similar message to the one Jesus gave his disciples after his resurrection. (Matt 28:18-20). The spirits are many. Jesus is one, and God is his Father.

Other differences between Christ's resurrection and the manifestation of spirits could be listed. There are quite a number. But it does not matter how many differences there are. We don't want to prove anything. It should suffice to know that the Kingdom of God and the realm of the spirits are completely different. They actually have nothing to do with one another.

As a Christian in the Lutheran tradition, I, like many other Protestants, have been shaped by the biblical Word and the guidance of God's Holy Spirit. Over and above that there have been preachers and teachers who have assisted me throughout my life. In one point, however, none of them have been able to convince me as much as Martin Luther has. By reading Luther's writings I have come to the conviction that there is no proof that life after death exists.

Luther lived in an age when spirits manifested themselves in all sections of society. During the Middle Ages, especially monks and nuns had nocturnal apparitions in their cloister rooms of their deceased religious brothers and sisters. Luther rejects these apparitions, saying that they have been sent by the devil. They are not from God. He says: "We need to be aware, and it is important to know that we are not alone, thinking that the devil is a hundred miles away from us. He is all around us and frequently disguises himself; as I have witnessed myself, he appears as a sow, a straw fire and suchlike. One needs to be aware of this; for it prevents us from turning these things into superstitions and deeming such spirits to be human souls; as has been hitherto the case, to the great benefit and elevation of the papal mass. All the world believed [these manifestations of the devil] to be human souls, as has been well testified ... But we unfortunately know only too well the terrible fallacies and idolatries to which they have subsequently given rise."[68] It is not known whether the spirits of

---

[68] Easter Sermon on Lk. 24:36-48, cf. Walch Band XIIIa, p. 529f. (This is not the official English translation of this Luther text, but the translator's own.) – 'Solches ist nutz und noth, daß mans wisse, daß wir nicht so allein sind, als wäre der Teufel über hundert Meilen Weges von uns. Er ist allenthalben um uns, und zieht bisweilen ein Larve an; wie ich selbst gesehen habe, daß er sich sehen läßt, als

the dead appeared to Luther himself. He was troubled by the devil and spirits and beset by poltergeists, more so than most people. This has been ascribed to Luther having attracted the devil and his spirits because of his faith and also his conflict with the Catholic church.

To this day the Catholic church views Martin Luther as having been a theologian with revolutionary and seditious intent, who believed in the devil and was accordingly influenced by him. One has to view Martin Luther in the context of his time. The end of the Middle Ages was filled with erroneous beliefs about witches and spirits. Luther had to deal with the superstitions of his age and the environment he lived in. There is no evidence that he ever succumbed to even one of the temptations of the devil that he was faced with. On the contrary: He addresses the devil with the personal "you" and refers and points him to Jesus who is stronger, or to Scripture.

By the way: E. Levi, a Catholic priest, has the following to say about Luther: "Superstitiously and audaciously, he deemed himself to be possessed by the devil. The devil dictated the arguments against the Church to him, allowed him to take issue and to say and especially write foolish things."[69] Because Luther's reformationist ideas were unacceptable to the then degenerate Church, he is grouped together with those who were possessed by the devil. Luther's writings paint a completely different picture: "Verily, the devil is still a prince in this world, and I have hitherto not escaped him. For as long as I reside in his princedom, however, I am not safe from him; therefore I must partake in the Sacrament to be near my beloved Reliever and Saviour, so that my heart and faith may be strengthened every day...".[70]

---

wäre er eine Sau, ein brennender Strohwisch, und dergleichen. Das muß man wissen, denn es dient uns dazu, daß wir keinen Aberglauben daraus machen und solche Geister nicht für Menschenseelen halten; ... Denn Jedermann hielt es dafür, es wären Menschenseelen; wie man daß gute Zeugnisse hat, ... Was aber daraus für gräuliche Intümer und Abgötterei gefolgt, wissen wir leider nur allzuviel.'

[69] Op. cit., p. 357. – 'Abergläubig und verwegen glaubte er sich vom Teufel besessen. Der Teufel diktierte ihm die Argumente gegen die Kirche, ließ ihm widersprechen, unvernünftig reden und vor allem schreiben.'

[70] Cf. Aland, 130. (This is not the official English translation of this Luther text, but the translator's own.) – 'Wahrlich, der Teufel ist noch ein Fürst in der Welt, und ich bin ihm noch nicht entronnen. Solange ich aber in seinem Fürstentum bin, bin ich

Luther was a theologian and teacher who, more than his contemporaries, was guided by Scripture. He was not the only one. Many people followed his example. In many cases these people aligned themselves with the apostle Paul.

One text of the apostle Paul speaks of life after death in a radical way. Paul refers to a verse from the Prophet Isaiah when he says: "If the dead are not raised, 'Let us eat and drink, for tomorrow we die'." (1 Kor 15:32). With this statement the apostle cannot give us proof of an afterlife either, but he firmly believes that Jesus Christ, his Lord, will raise him from the dead. Paul can live with this certainty of faith. Whatever happens in eternity is in God's power, together with the angels and heavenly hosts that surround Him.

Through Christ's resurrection we are promised a life after death (John 11:25-26; 14:19). By believing in our Lord, we as Christians have a good idea of the eternal world of God we will share with Him. Evil, as well as all spirits returning to earth, will not be with God. It does not matter whether these spirits are those created and conjured up by magical means, or those imaginary ones that pretend to impart something to this world from the other side.

---

vor ihm nicht sicher, deshalb muß ich zum Sakrament gehen und mich zu meinem lieben Helfer und Heiland halten, damit mein Herz und Glaube täglich gestärkt werde ...'.

Beauty and purity as a symbol of God's good creation.

The traditional world view of the *Batswana*

Modimo = God

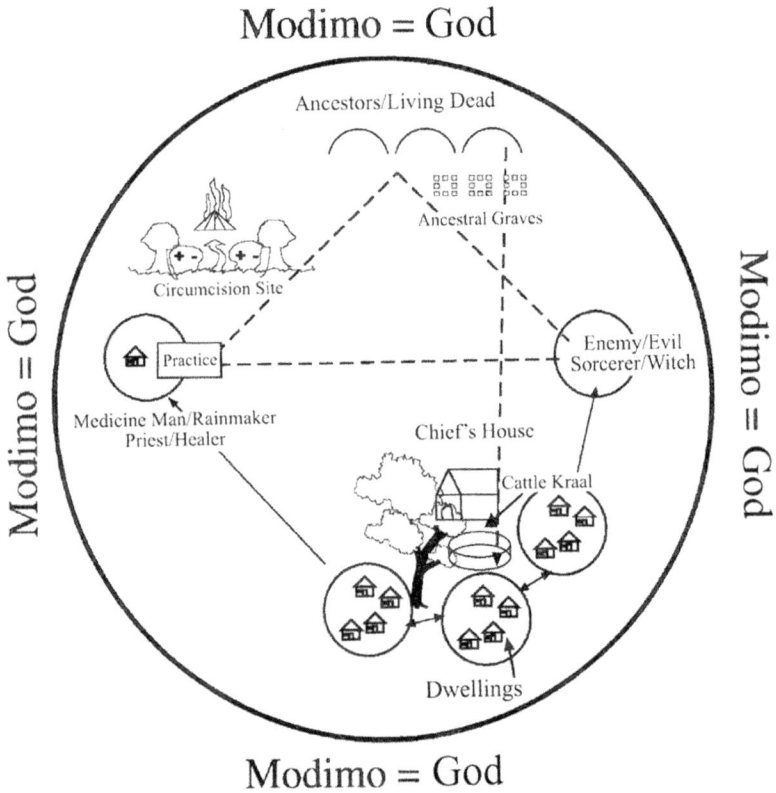

Having been placed all around the outside circumference of the circle, *Modimo* points to the omnipotence of God, which overlooks all life within the circle, giving it strength. *Modimo* is depicted as the all-encompassing deity. At the same time the circle only represents a symbolic boundary.

The triangular connection at the centre of the diagram represents the meeting point of power, the ancestors. They keep the other two powers under surveillance. The people living in their settlements – symbolised by the houses – are making their supplications and requests to the three places of power. In turn and in equal measure, the centres of power have an effect on the people, the livestock and the homesteads.

Bibliography

Aland, K., *Die Werke Martin Luthers*, Vol. VI. Stuttgart: Ehrenfried Klotz, [2]1966.

Alcock, J.E. *Parapsychology, Science or Magic? A Psychological Perspective.* Oxford: Pergamon Press, 1981.

Alverson, H. *Mind in the Heart of Darkness – Value and Self-Identity among the Tswana of Southern Africa.* Cape Town: McMillan, 1978.

Bammann, H., *Geistererscheinungen und magische Inszenierungen aus phänomenologischen Fallstudien im Kontext des südafrikanischen Welt-bildes mit religionsgeschichtlichen und anthropologischen Analysen, pa-rapsychologischen Begriffsbestimmungen und einem christlich-theologischen Ausblick.* Hermannsburg: Ludwig-Harms-Haus, 2014.

Bammann, H., *Geisterphänomene in Afrika.* In: Evangelikale Missiologie 3/2004: 100-108.

Baurichter, K., *Glaube, Spuk und Gestalten. Ein Sagenkranz aus der Lüne-burger Heide verflochten mit Geschichte und Edda-Sagen.* Ed.: Heimat-bund Kreis Soltau e.V., 1954.

Bender, H. (ed.), *Parapsychologie: Entwicklung, Ergebnisse, Probleme.* Darmstadt: Wissenschaftliche Buchgemeinschaft, 1974.

Beth, K., *Das Verhältnis von Magie und Religion.* In Petzold: 27-46, 1978.

Bosch, D.J., *The Problem of Evil in Africa: A Survey of African Views of Witchcraft and of the Response of the Christian Church.* In: *Like a Roar-ing Lion: Essays on the Bible, the Church, and Demonic Powers*, Pieter G.R. de Villiers (ed.), Pretoria: UNISA, 1987, p. 38-62.

Bucher, H. *Spirits and Power – An Analysis of Shona Cosmology.* Cape Town: Oxford University Press, 1980.

Ellens, J.H. *Psychotheology: Key Issues.* Pretoria: University of South Africa, 1987.

Eysenck, J./Sargent, C. *Explaining the unexplained – Mysteries of the para-normal.* London: Weidenfeld and Nicolson, 1982.

Farsen, D., *Ghosts in fact and fiction.* London: Hamlin, 1980.

Finucane, R.C. *Appearences oft he dead – A cultural history of ghosts.* Lon-don: Junction Books, 1982.

Gerding, J.L. *Exceptional human experiences: Philosophical, psychological and parapsychological perspectives*, in Wulfhorst: 23-40, 2004.

Haag, H., *Vor dem Bösen ratlos?* München/Zürich: Piper, 1989.

Häselbarth, H., *Die Auferstehung der Toten in Afrika. Eine theologische Deutung der Todesriten der Mamabolo in Nordtransvaal.* Gütersloh: Gütersloher Verlagshaus, 1972.

Hummel, R., *Reinkarnation. Weltbilder des Reinkarnationsglaubens und das Christentum.* Mainz: Matthias Grünewald / Stuttgart: Quell, 1989.

Irvine, D., *From Witchcraft to Christ.* Hothorpe Hall: Concordia Press, 1983.

Janzen, W., *Okkultismus. Erscheinungen, übersinnliche Kräfte, Spiritismus.* Mainz: Matthias Grünewald / Stuttgart: Quell, 1988. Ad. E., *Gibt es Zauberhandlungen?* In Petzold: 279-295, 1978.

Jung, C.G., *Die Beziehungen zwischen dem Ich und dem Unbewußten.* Jung, L. (ed.), München: dtv, 1990.

Jung, C.G., *Typologie.* Jung, L. (ed.), München: dtv, 1990.

Jung, C.G., *Traum und Traumdeutung.* Jung, L. (ed.), München: dtv, 1990.

Jung, C.G., *Synchronizität, Akausalität und Okkultismus.* Jung, L. (ed.), München: dtv, 1990.

Kgasi, M. *Thuto ke eng?* Lovedale: Lovedale Press, 1949.

Kgatla, S.T. *Mmoloi ga a nna mmala (a which has no colour) – Witchcraft accusations in South Africa*, in Missionalia 1/2004: 84-101.

Koch, K., *Seelsorge und Okkultismus. Eine Untersuchung unter Berücksichtigung der Inneren Medizin, Psychiatrie, Psychologie, Tiefenpsychologie, Religionspsychologie, Parapsychologie, Theologie.* Berghausen: Evangelisationsverlag, 1959.

Lee, R., *Beware the Devil. A True Story of Deliverance from Evil.* Aylesbury: Marshall, Morgan and Scott, 1983.

Levi, E., *Geschichte der Magie.* Basel: Sphinx, 1985.

Lewis-Williams, D./Pearce, D. *Sun spirituality – Roots, expressions and social consequences.* Cape Town: Double Story Books, 2004.

Magoleng, B.D. *Ke a go bolela.* Pretoria: JL van Schalk, 1974.

Mbiti, J.S., *Concepts of God in Africa.* London: S.P.C.K., 1971.

Mbiti, J.S. *African Religions and Philosophy.* London/Ibadan/Nairobi: Heinemann, 1971.

Mönnig, H.O., *The Pedi*. Pretoria: J.L. van Schaik. [2]1983.

Moser, F., *Spuk in neuer Sicht*. In Bender: 524-542, 1974.

Ntsime, J.M. *Pelo e ntsho*. Boodwood: Via Africa, 1979.

Ntsime, J.M./Rousseau, G.J./Mampie, P.A. *Matlhasedi a bobedi*. Goodwood: Via Africa.

Pettersson, O., *Magie-Religion. Eine Randbemerkung zu einem alten Problem*. In Petzold: 313-324, 1978.

Petzold, L. (ed.), *Magie und Religion – Beiträge zu einer Theorie der Magie*. Darmstadt: Wissenschaftliche Buchgesellschaft, 1978.

Richter, G.and E., *Der afrikanische Heiler*. In Lutherische Mission in Südafrika: 66-76. Bammann, H. (ed.), Ev.-Luth. Missionswerk in Niedersachsen, 1990.

Schapera, I. Mekgwa le melao ya *Batswana*. Lovedale: Lovedale Press.

Schnurr, O., *Aberglaube. Faszination und Versuchung*. München: Kösel, 1988.

Schutte, A.G., *Thapelo ya Sephiri. A Study of Secret Prayer Groups in Soweto*. African Studies 31.4.1972: 245-260, 1972.

Seiling, M., *Goethe als Esoteriker*. Hardo, T. (ed.), Melsbach/Neuwied: "Die Silberschnur", 1988.

Setiloane, G.M., *The Image of God among the Sotho-Tswana*. Rotterdam: AA Balkema, 1976.

Tswana hymnal 1987, *Kopelo ya Kereke ya Luthere*. Rustenburg: Lutheran Book Depot, 1979, reprint 1993.

Vielliers, P.G. (ed.) *Like a roaring lion ... Essays on the Bible, the church and demonic powers*. Pretoria: University of South Africa, 1987.

Walch 2, J.G., *Dr. Martin Luthers sämtliche Schriften*. Vol. III. St Louis: Concordia Publishing House, 1892.

Walch 2, J.G., *Dr. Martin Luthers sämtliche Schriften*. Vol. XIIIa. St Louis: Concordia Publishing House, 1904.

Wax, M.and R., *Der Begriff der Magie*. In Petzold: 325-384, 1978.

Wenisch, B., *Satanismus: Schwarze Messen, Dämonenglaube, Hexenkulte*. Mainz: Matthias Grünewald / Stuttgart: Quell, 1988.

Wulfhorst, I. (ed.), *Spiritualism: A challenge of the Churches in Europe*. Geneva: Lutheran World Federation.

www.ingramcontent.com/pod-product-compliance
Lightning Source LLC
LaVergne TN
LVHW021404080426
835508LV00020B/2447